MW00582333

This book is dedicated to the storytellers who have influenced and inspired me. DFKY wouldn't exist without each of you.

Aaron S.

Aja A.

Alan R.

Alexis S.

Anthony B.

Bo B.

Chris W.

Hayley W.

James B.

John L.

Jonathan L.

Lane M.

Lin-Manuel M.

Mike B.

Natalie C.

Odette Y.

Rachel W., Susan L., and the teens of VOX Teen Communications

Ron M.

Susan H.

Vera and Clyde R.

In memory of those lost to suicide

Steven William Romig
November 4, 1948–February 24, 1996

A crowd-funding campaign was held in early 2021 to raise money to publish this book. Each donor was invited to share a name or initials of a loved one lost to suicide. These are their people, and a few more whose lives impacted me. They all left us far too soon. Rest in peace to each of them.

Anthony Bourdain
Bill Davidson
Chantal Akerman
Chris Cornell
Cliff Vaughn
DW
Dale Bertrand
Dan Williams
Davis Beasley
GK, JH, & JW
Hank Tanner
J. D. Blagg
Jean Seberg
Jeremy Reynolds
John Hendricks
Johnathan
Julia Keller

Kenny McKinley
Kristin Foss
Kurt Cobain
Marti Schimmel
Matt Rog
Michael Ferguson
Michelle Ferguson Priestly
Michael Garrot
Dr. Michael E. King
RWL
Randy Seals
Robin Williams
S
Solomon Chase
Terri Mahoney
Tierra Spruill
Tim Cunningham

A percentage of DFKY's proceeds will go to support Suicide Survival Stories, a nonprofit designed to create suicide-related conversation to help struggling humans stay alive, and keep those who died alive through storytelling. Learn more at www.suicidesurvivalstories.org.

ADDITIONAL SUICIDE AWARENESS AND PREVENTION RESOURCES

The Giving Kitchen partners with the QPR Institute to provide free training to food service workers nationwide. QPR stands for Question, Persuade, and Refer—three steps anyone can learn to prevent suicide. Read more about QPR at www.qprinstitute.com, and about The Giving Kitchen at www.thegivingkitchen.org. If you're a restaurant worker, you can take the 45-minute course for FREE online at www.thegivingkitchen.org/qpr.

The American Foundation for Suicide Prevention (AFSP) gives those affected by suicide a nationwide community empowered by research, education, and advocacy to take action against this leading cause of death. Visit www.afsp.org/suicide-prevention-resources for emergency resources, crisis services, and mental health care information.

Crisis Text Line provides free, 24/7, high-quality text-based mental health support and crisis intervention by empowering a community of trained volunteers to support people in their moments of need. Text HOME to 741741 to connect with a Crisis Counselor or visit www.crisistextline.org for more information or to volunteer to become a trained crisis counselor.

RAINN (Rape, Abuse & Incest National Network) is the nation's largest anti-sexual violence organization. Visit hotline.rainn.org/online to chat online with a trained staff member who can provide you with confidential crisis support. You can also visit volopps.rainn.org to find volunteer opportunities at a RAINN–Partner Crisis Center in your area.

The Trevor Project is the leading national organization providing crisis intervention and suicide prevention services to lesbian, gay, bisexual, transgender, queer, and questioning (LGBTQ) young people under the age of 25. For immediate support, please call the TrevorLifeline at 1-866-488-7386 or select TrevorChat at www.thetrevorproject.org/get-help-now/ to connect with a counselor.

Don't F*cking Kill Yourself

A Memoir of Suicide, Survival,
and Stories That Keep Us Alive

JEFF ROMIG

HOUNDSTOOTH
PRESS

The information presented herein represents the views of the author as of the date of publication. This book is presented for informational purposes only. Due to the rate at which conditions change, the author reserves the right to alter and update his opinions based on new conditions. While every attempt has been made to verify the information in this book, neither the author nor his affiliates/partners assume any responsibility for errors, inaccuracies, or omissions.

 HOUNDSTOOTH
PRESS

DON'T F*CKING KILL YOURSELF
A Memoir of Suicide, Survival, and Stories That Keep Us Alive

ISBN   PAPERBACK: 978-1-5445-2365-1
         EBOOK: 978-1-5445-2364-4

CONTENTS

Advance Praise

February 23, 1996

I TRIED TO WATCH *The Big Chill* when I was 18, but I fell asleep before Marvin Gaye finished singing "I Heard It Through the Grapevine," minutes into the movie.

At 36, I would finally watch the entire film, but not without thinking about this Friday night in 1996, when I chose it as my escape from the world, instead of a more familiar flick.

Sometimes these things choose us.

My parents had bought that VHS tape years before, but I'd never been interested in it. It simply filled a slot on the shelf, alongside worn favorites of mine like *The Outsiders*, *Top Gun*, and *Ferris Bueller's Day Off*. For my parents, the story was a moment frozen in time, evoking their younger years through melancholy and music. I didn't know the plot, nor did I take the time to learn more from the back of its sleeve.

I'd begun the evening at Spring Valley High School, working to wrap up the current issue of *The Viking Shield*. As on most Fridays, I'd made no plans. Once I left my high school newspaper colleagues, I would simply hide in my bedroom from everyone and everything.

I deeply wanted my life to change.

I'd turned 18 on February 7. Now, technically an "adult," I mistakenly believed I was ready for anything. In three months, I'd graduate and finally leave Columbia, SC, on my way to college—six hours west at The University of Alabama in Tuscaloosa, I hoped.

The NBA trade deadline had been earlier that day, which only mattered because Dad used it as an attempt to engage me as he sat at the kitchen table, writing on his laptop.

"Did you see that Christian Laettner was traded to Atlanta?" he asked, as I grabbed a Coca-Cola from the fridge at around 10 p.m. I barely acknowledged the question about the former Duke star, or my dad's existence: "Saw that," I mumbled as I headed upstairs, rebuffing his attempt to connect.

Why was he trying to talk to me? Conversation hadn't been part of our father-son dynamic since I'd become an angsty, sarcastic teen. I didn't want to talk basketball. I didn't want to make chit-chat. I just wanted to be left alone.

Maybe we'd talk tomorrow. Tonight, I wanted to watch this movie—which I didn't know was about baby boomers reuniting in Beaufort, SC to mourn their friend who had died by suicide.

But I wouldn't watch *The Big Chill* that night. I'd drift off to sleep instead. By the time I actually saw it in full for the first time as a 36-year-old, I'd lived almost two more decades, completely shaped by the tragedy that preceded my 13-year-old brother's screams around 6:30 a.m. on Saturday, February 24, 1996.

"Get up! Dad killed himself!"

January 16, 1991

WE COULDN'T HEAR what the CNN anchor was saying over the crack of the pool balls echoing across Opening Break, a pool hall and restaurant in downtown Columbia. But as I took a bite of my honey-mustard-covered fried chicken finger, the Middle East map with Iraq in red on the wall-sized TV screen caught my eye.

Dad and I paused our game to watch as CNN delivered the news that Operation Desert Storm had begun with an aerial bombing campaign to drive Iraqi forces out of Kuwait.

Moments earlier, my biggest worry had been Dad kicking my ass in pool yet again.

But now, our country was at war.

After Dad paid our bill, we left our favorite pool-shooting spot on the University of South Carolina (USC) campus in downtown Columbia. Our next stop was the Carolina Coliseum (where I would ultimately graduate from high school, study journalism in its basement, and receive my bachelor's degree) to watch star guard Jo Jo English and the Gamecocks take on Virginia Tech in men's basketball.

Leading up to tip-off, we all prayed for the troops before we sang the national anthem. The Gamecocks won, which in the 1980s and 1990s wasn't a likely proposition.

I would turn 13 in less than a month, and this evening of losing at pool to my dad as the first non-cold war of my lifetime began would, strangely, be one of my last positive memories of him, and, more broadly, of our relationship during my teen years.

My IQ had put me with the "talented and gifted" kids in second grade, but I had coasted until the beginning of this year, seventh grade, when I began to lose interest in doing any more than the bare minimum academically. This infuriated him.

While math and science became perplexing, writing was still effortless. I enjoyed it, and that natural skill was the only part of school that gave me confidence. Reading sports stories every morning in *The State*, Columbia's daily newspaper, paired with watching *Beverly Hills 90210*'s Brandon Walsh and Andrea Zuckerman as high school journalists for the *Beverly Hills Blaze* on Thursday nights, was all that the 12-year-old version of me had needed to dream of being a newspaper reporter.

But, in the fall of 1990, I'd mainly cared about TV, movies, video games, girls, and sports—most of all my true love, baseball. The more my dad became angry when I didn't "meet my potential" on tests and report cards in middle school, the more I'd resisted making any change in my predisposed patterns.

Dad had even bought me the VHS series, *Where There's a Will There's an A*. But I didn't watch it.

I'd chosen instead to take a "Cs get degrees" approach to school, because I'd cared infinitely more about watching Ryne Sandberg play second base for the Cubs in afternoon games on WGN or staying up late for Chris Myers to tell me all about that day's games on *Baseball Tonight,* or re-watching *The Monster Squad*, *Side Out*, *Toy Soldiers*, or *Welcome Home, Roxy Carmichael* on my HBO-recorded VHS tapes.

I'd just wanted to watch and play baseball. And I dreamed of having a girlfriend like Winona Ryder's Dinky Bossetti. Dinky seemed not to fit in with the world in her and Roxy Carmichael's shared hometown of Clyde, Ohio, just as I was beginning to feel that I didn't fit into mine.

I definitely hadn't wanted to study whatever math, science, or revisionist Southern history they were force-feeding us in seventh grade at E. L. Wright Middle School in Northeast Columbia. This didn't sit well with Dad. Nothing I did pleased him: I should've earned better grades. I should've played tennis instead of baseball. And I should've been "grateful for the things he gave me."

No matter what, whatever I did, it wasn't good enough, wasn't right, wasn't in line with his expectations. At least this was the story I told myself then—and continued to, after his death.

Constantly trying to prove myself to Dad was toxic and emotionally exhausting when he was alive, yet I stubbornly continued to play that game, allowing the words from his suicide letter to define my self-talk.

Unlike most of my teammates' dads, he'd attended my baseball games infrequently. He missed my first legit, over-the-fence home run in the spring of 1991 because he left early after he ran into a tennis buddy at the ballpark, and they went across the street to play tennis.

After he missed that home run, I gave up on him, because I believed he'd given up on me.

In contrast to the ups and downs of my teen years, my memories from the 1980s of Dad, and of us together, are mainly positive ones.

The scars were simpler then.

I burned my left ring finger during our Saturday-morning father-son pancake routine. The inch-long dash in the middle of my forehead came from our nightly game when he came home from work, in which I'd charge him, and he'd dodge me like a matador; that game ended for good after my four-year-old forehead slammed into the corner of the table behind our couch, resulting in my first emergency-room trip and set of stitches.

Mostly, we had fun when I was a little kid. In 1983, we saw the first two original *Star Wars* films when they were re-released in theaters alongside *The Return of the Jedi*. We played *The Oregon Trail, Whistler's Brother*, and other games on the Commodore 64 computer he was so excited to buy us. We drove the three hours to Atlanta once a year in the late 1980s to watch unwatchable Braves baseball teams and eat at Hard Rock Café. We went to Myrtle Beach each summer for the Pavilion, fried shrimp, mini golf, and shark's tooth hunting on the beach.

When I think of the 1980s, I see his warm, broad smile. But the 1990s were quite different. And so were the scars.

Things were changing. On November 9, 1989, five days after his 41st birthday, communism and the Wall had fallen in his birthplace, Berlin. The 1990s were less than two months away; my terrible middle-school years had begun two months before; and unbeknownst to any of us, Dad was entering the final years of his life, as his mental illness worked to destroy him.

But Steve Romig was a fighter.

After his family moved back to Germany in 1966 on a US Army transfer, he decided to return to the United States on his own to finish his senior year at Richmond Academy in Augusta, Georgia, where they'd previously been living. My aunt Joan, who was in seventh grade herself when Dad left for the US, remembered their father telling Dad, "When you live in my house you follow my rules, but once you are 18, you can move out and do whatever you want." So, after Dad turned 18 on November 4, 1966, he left.

"I thought that this was the worst thing that ever happened to me," Joan wrote to me.

Dad then put himself through Augusta College, where he excelled in the classroom and on the tennis court. There he became study buddies with my maternal grandmother Vera, who had gone back to school to earn her degree.

Vera introduced him to her oldest daughter Sandra. He and Sandra began dating and were married in June of 1971. With my mom's modest elementary school teacher's salary and his job selling suits at Sears paying the bills, Dad earned his Juris Doctorate from USC in 1975.

I think his biggest frustration about me was that I inherited most of his intelligence but none of the drive, discipline, and resilience that were key to his success.

Ironically, I only developed those traits in the wake of his death, as I learned, painfully, to navigate my inherited mental health challenges and the lessons of his suicide.

Today

ABOUT 10 YEARS ago, a friend asked me what I'd say to my dad if I could only say one more thing to him.

I immediately answered: "Don't fucking kill yourself."

If today, you are thinking about killing yourself, I'm saying the same thing to you. And I'm saying it to myself.

I hope the stories in this book help pull you through your own dark moments by sparking the recognition of your passions, people, and experiences for long enough to help you stay alive despite the persistent, incessant pain you might be feeling.

I know this pain too.

I also know that pushing through our darkness is how we survive. I've learned to stay alive in those moments by reconnecting with my passions, people, and experiences.

Thus far, I've survived car wrecks, my father's suicide, divorce, cancer, alcoholism, a global pandemic, and other difficulties you'll read about—all while fighting through a maelstrom of anxiety, depression, and suicidal ideation (which is defined as thinking about, considering, or planning suicide).

But, despite my resilience, my biggest fear is that the final words I'll ever write will be in my suicide letter.

As a writer, words are my superpower. But, as a writer and a human being who has to fight chronic anxiety and depression, words are also my Kryptonite.

On a daily basis, the negative words in my mind—and all kinds of words said to me by others—could potentially put my life in danger, but the truth is our stories don't have to end at our own hands.

Regardless of how our deep wounds or dark thoughts might manipulate us into the suicidal ideas and planning that can precede an attempt to make our pain stop forever, *we are in control.* I believe that in those life-and-death moments of free fall, our parachute is the ability to reconnect with our stories. They can keep us alive, if we just remember them.

For 25 years, my mental illness has tricked me into believing I'm walking my dad's path.

A path of depression.

A path of brokenness.

A path of inevitability.

His path led him into a gray 1987 Volvo station wagon filled with carbon monoxide, ending his life after 47 years, three months, and 20 days of fighting a war—which was unwinnable alone—against the aberrant chemical reactions inside his brain that contributed to his suicide. This is my take on his mind, based on his final act and the words in his suicide letters. He and I hadn't been close for years when he died, 17 days after my 18th birthday. We were very alike, yet very different.

Dad was never diagnosed, but I have been.

I believe our shared DNA bestowed upon us both intelligence, introversion, generalized anxiety, and clinical depression. But I don't believe he ever knew most of these attributes existed in him, because men of his generation didn't go to therapy or take antidepressants or talk about their feelings much at all. To my knowledge, he never did any of those things, or told anyone he was struggling—until he wrote his suicide letters.

That's why it was a brutal shock.

The day of Dad's suicide, I decided to do everything I could to be different from him, even though I didn't have any comprehension of anxiety or depression, or that those diseases had already been gestating inside me since middle school.

I was 18, in shock, and unbelievably angry. But in those first fatherless hours, I committed to always talking about whatever insanity was going through my mind, so I wouldn't find myself on the path that led him to his death.

That commitment seemed simple. But mental illness is not simple. It's complex, insidious, and potentially deadly.

Now 43, I've been on prescribed anxiety and depression meds for 19 years, and consistently in therapy for 14 years, but I still struggle daily to live a life free of the complications these diseases create.

While navigating my dysfunctional mind, I've found success and experienced failure as a newspaper journalist, nonprofit executive and fundraiser, and political campaign manager and strategist.

I've learned through not just successes, but through mistakes, ignorance, and selfishness.

And I've had to remind myself daily that the only way I can grow from and make amends for my failures is by staying alive.

Our flawed, fun house-mirror minds will try to catastrophize each of our screw-ups as a justifiable reason to end our lives. But the penalty for our mistakes shouldn't be death at our own hands. We will only become the people we want to be, and live the lives we envision for ourselves, if we push through our excruciating pain and stay alive.

Throughout my three careers, I've often wondered how insanely difficult it must have been for my dad to stay alive until 47 with no medication, no therapy, and no realization or understanding of the disease grinding away at his sanity, minute after minute, day after day, year after year.

I still wonder what he was thinking in his final conscious minutes, as the carbon monoxide invaded his lungs and seeped into his brain. How, with time to think, could he execute his plan?

Why didn't he realize the mistake he was making, tear up the letters he wrote, and slip back into bed instead of throwing so many lives into chaos?

The end of his suffering sparked infinite pain for so many people, and these unanswerable questions still haunt me.

But one that can be answered is how long he was awake in that car. It takes around five minutes to lose consciousness from concentrated carbon monoxide in that small a space.

I think about his final 300 seconds a lot.

In theory, the adrenaline response when facing death has the effect of slowing time. You think in hyper speed, creating the sensation of life flashing before your eyes. I can only imagine what memories from his 47 years he may have seen. And if happy memories came to him, why couldn't he foil his own plan? Maybe it was simply too late?

That's why I wrote this book. Its stories include memories of passions, people, and experiences I think I'd see if my life flashed before my eyes. Some are painful. Some memories are happy. Some are heartbreaking. Some are incredibly difficult to revisit. They're not shared chronologically, since our lives probably wouldn't flash in front of our eyes chronologically. But they collectively make me who I am—an incredibly flawed human trying daily to be the best version of myself.

Remembering my stories helps me stay alive. And I want to remain connected to these memories, so that I'm never in the position that he ended up in as he died in that Volvo. And I want to share them with you, so that my stories might facilitate a connection within you to your own passions, people, and experiences.

Maybe, instead of Hayley Williams of Paramore, your favorite musical storyteller is Tupac Shakur, or Garth Brooks. Maybe you revere President Reagan. Maybe the sports moment etched in your mind is Colin Kaepernick kneeling, or Brandi Chastain's World Cup-winning penalty kick, or Dale Earnhardt's death at Daytona. Maybe you collect coins, or records, or guns, or political campaign buttons, or recipes. Maybe your Sunday lunches include lasagna or biryani or groundnut stew instead of fried okra, butter beans, cornbread, and barbecue chicken. Maybe watching a football match brings you the joy that a baseball game gives me.

The likeliest of scenarios is that you'll see parallels I'd never even imagine, because maybe our only connection is a shared struggle with anxiety, depression, and suicidal ideas.

In myriad moments (or incessantly), you may think things are hopeless for you. But I'm here to say that maybe, just maybe, that's not true.

Here's what is true. You are resilient. You are loved. You have value. And you have stories that are worth building upon, rather than leaving behind in a mushroom cloud of devastation for the people who love you.

We shouldn't judge our insides by someone else's outside; despite what a person reveals or projects, no one can fully understand their daily internal struggle. Everyone has their shit. But for those of us experiencing mental illness, our problems can feel all-consuming as they push us into the dark corners of our minds and worlds, desperate for reprieve.

Suicide is a global epidemic, with approximately 800,000 people dying by their own hand annually, according to the World Health Organization. These statistics predate the COVID-19 global pandemic. We aren't likely to understand the mental health impact of 2020–2021 for years.

But our diseases, problems, and failures do not define us.

We're not the trauma we've experienced, and we're not the diseases we battle. We're not our feelings or our thoughts or our neuroses. And we're not our mistakes.

But we *are* our lessons learned, and the changes we implement in response.

We're our people, passions, and experiences. And the impact they've had on our minds and lives can help us stay alive through our most graphic suicidal ideas.

I'm not formally trained in psychology or psychiatry. I'm not a therapist or a counselor. And this isn't a self-help book.

I don't believe there is any silver bullet or magical solution to prevent suicide, but I hope that, by writing this memoir, the stories I share will help you understand that you're not alone.

The world needs us and our stories. And most importantly, the people in our stories need and want us to be alive and healthy, regardless of the deception delivered by our self-talk. My depression tries to con me into believing the worst possible scenario, and I feel alone so much of the time. But writing this has reminded me that even when I think I'm alone, I'm really not. In my lowest lows, the passions, people, and experiences that have shaped my life remind me how close I am to the connections I crave.

On the mornings when my paralyzing depression traps me in bed or the afternoons when my anxiety manifests in panic attacks or the nights when my suicidal ideation wants me to end my life, the stories shared in these pages remind me of what's been and what could be if, during these dark moments, I trick the part of my mind that wants to kill me.

I believe your stories will do the same for you.

That's why I'm sharing this non-linear story about my journey: to prove that you and I aren't alone—despite how much we have convinced ourselves of that lie.

This book is about suicide and survival. It's about success, utter failure, and changing to recover and learn from both. It's about the passions, people, and experiences that define the stories that help keep us alive, and it's about hope, perspective, and pushing through pain and fear.

These things keep me alive. They can for you, too.

July 28, 1992

I CRAWLED UP THE 45-degree chipped and cracked limestone steps one by one, gripping the rusty, thick-linked chain to my left. It had been placed on this almost 1,200-year-old pyramid for the exact purpose of keeping tentative tourists from tumbling backward down the 91-step stairway.

El Castillo—also known as the Temple of Kukulcán—is the heart of the Mayan city of Chichen Itza. The sum of the 91 steps in each of the stairways on the pyramid's four sides, plus the temple on its top platform, equals the 365 days of the Mayan calendar.

We'd arrived an hour earlier, after a hot, bumpy, three-hour bus ride from our resort hotel in Cancun, which sits at the northeastern tip of Mexico's Yucatán Peninsula.

But that journey was nothing compared to this steep climb. And now it was starting to rain.

Mom, along with my 10-year-old brother Bryan, had attempted the climb, but had made the smart choice to return to the ground, where her white Keds were now about to be destroyed by the mud created by the storm.

I was already two-thirds of the way up, so I set my focus on the highest, final step, sped up, and rose to my feet at the top in front of the temple only seconds before the bottom fell out of the sky, drenching everyone still climbing, and ensuring that the climb down would be much more treacherous than the climb up had been.

Standing inside the temple—a small, dark room—I peered through the downpour to take in the entire set of ruins in a single, breathtaking view. The Temple of the Warriors and its 200 flanking square columns were off to my right; to my left sat The Great Ball Court, where the losing captain would typically be decapitated for his failure. Yikes.

It was a moment I'd never forget, and it had almost never happened. Had all gone well, I would have been in America, playing baseball. But it hadn't, and so I owed this once-in-a-lifetime moment to a super-talented kid named Brian, a rising sophomore, who had taken the mound as the starting pitcher for his West Columbia All-Star team in back-to-back games of a best-of-three series, and totally shut down the bats of my Northeast Columbia All-Star team.

Our team of rising high school freshmen had played together for a little more than a month after the Pony League regular season ended. We were one of two Northeast Columbia All-Star teams in a dual-bracketed tournament, which meant that the two sub-district winners would face off in this series for the opportunity to represent Columbia in the state championship tournament.

Our scrappy team hadn't been the most talented in the sub-district tournament, but we'd had a few great players (Fish, Dan, Kent, and Scott), an excellent coach, and more heart than the rest of the field combined. That had been enough to beat our rival Northeast Columbia team and make it to the final. And it had been more than enough to best the Lower Richland boys. That win had given us the opportunity to get totally shut down by the right arm and wicked curveball of this Brian kid, who later went on to pitch at The Citadel before being a Boston Red Sox draftee.

When we were in the midst of that run, grinding out inning after inning in 101-degree Columbia heat, Mayan ruins had been the farthest thing from my mind. If we had won, we wouldn't have gone on this trip—or at least I wouldn't have gone. And I would have missed so much quality time with my family, since we didn't typically spend six consecutive days in the same room together.

During the daytime, I'd done my own thing at the resort, whether swimming in the ocean, shooting pool for hours, listening to Pearl Jam's *Ten* over and over on my Sony Discman, or discovering new foods, like the chilled sweet-and-sour gazpacho that I ate multiple times during our stay.

But at night, in the midst of the Barcelona Olympics and the baseball season, my dad and I had watched sports together, which wasn't exactly a routine of ours. The year before, I'd begged for—and finally received—a 20-inch Sony television for my bedroom, and I'd watched most sports either with friends, in our den or theirs, or alone in my room.

But on this trip, Dad and I had been able to share some fun sports memories, even if they hadn't involved me playing second base in the state tournament.

The previous Saturday, we'd stopped in Savannah as the halfway point before we flew to Cancun from Florida. That night, in our room, we'd watched in awe as Braves centerfielder Otis Nixon had climbed the right-centerfield wall, like a spider-bitten Peter Parker, to rob Andy Van Slyke of a home run in the ninth inning of a game the Braves won 1–0. TBS had kept replaying "the catch," and we'd talked about Skip Carey's call for days: "He caught the ball! He caught the ball! I can't believe it! What a catch by Otis Nixon! He took a home run away!"

Then on Sunday night, we'd watched Twins star Kirby Puckett drive in three runs to lead Minnesota to an 8–2 win over Boston at Fenway Park. It was a pretty run-of-the-mill game, but it was the first sporting event I'd ever experienced in Spanish. And the afternoon before our trip to Chichen Itza, we'd watched Michael Jordan and the Dream Team put on a clinic to beat the Croatian National Team 103–70 on their way to run away with the Gold for the United States.

Until this moment, at the top of this ancient pyramid, I'd never felt more alive than when I took my spot on the edge of the grass at second base while playing baseball.

I'd ducked into the small, dark temple to find a dry spot and surprisingly ran into Dad, who'd climbed up the other side.

As we stood on the top of the world together, peering through the deluge, I knew that I would never trade the memories I'd created with my dad over the previous few days in exchange for playing ball.

June 11, 1999

I JUMPED OUT OF the cab at the corner of North Clark and West Addison Streets and raced toward the ballpark I'd dreamed about visiting since I was a middle-school kid watching Cubs stars Ryne Sandberg, Shawon Dunston, and Mark Grace turn double plays most afternoons on WGN.

I was at Wrigley Field in Chicago. Finally.

But, because of a delayed flight, I was late. Late for the most important appointment of my life. And I hated to be late.

To make things worse, my brother had had to take a separate cab from O'Hare to drop our bags at the Days Inn before joining me. It was Bryan's 17th birthday. We had no cell phones, and he didn't have a credit card.

The prospect of hearing Mom scold me for "losing my little brother in Chicago" was all I could think about.

Compounding my anxiety was the thrilling but terrifying fact that I wasn't just at Wrigley as a fan: I had my pen. I had my reporter's notebook. I had my microcassette recorder, and I had my press pass.

On this Friday, even though I'd just finished my junior year in college and was only 21, I was there to write a story on Chicago Cubs General Manager Ed Lynch, who'd pitched for USC on the

Gamecocks' 1977 College World Series team before going on to work 940⅓ innings for the New York Mets and the Chicago Cubs between 1980 and 1987.

I glided through Wrigley's dark, dingy corridors, eventually finding my way to the 85-year-old cathedral's steep, concrete staircase—which led to one of the most thrilling moments of my life.

As I reached the top of the steps, my anxiety briefly disappeared as I became entranced by the ivy, the bleachers, and the history. I took a deep breath, composed myself, and walked down the aisle toward the field.

My press credential was an all-access pass to my childhood.

Before I stepped onto the dirt and then the grass for the first time, I took a minute to truly soak in everything around me. I could smell the aromas of Italian beef with giardiniera and Old Style beer wafting through the air. I could hear the buzz of the first fans, who'd arrived early to see the Cubs take on the cross-town rival White Sox. And I could feel the history of Tinker to Evers to Chance, Ernie Banks playing two, the Sandberg Game in June 1984, and Kerry Wood's unbelievable 20-strikeout game only 13 months before.

So many moments. So much love for the Cubbies and their home. Now I was standing in the park that always seemed a world away from my TV.

I stepped down and walked toward the grass, wishing I could take off my shoes and make "fists wit my toes," John McClane-style, to feel the grass on my skin, like Bruce Willis did to calm his anxiety in my favorite Christmas movie, *Die Hard*.

And I gazed out at second base, dreaming of taking a round of infield ground balls on the same patch of grass and dirt where Sandberg, my baseball hero, had played Gold Glove defense throughout his 16-year Hall of Fame career.

Then it hit me. I was late! So I stopped daydreaming and found the press contact, who told me to wait in the dugout. Ed Lynch would be there to meet me shortly, and I could interview any other players I wanted in the meantime.

So I waited. And I worried about Bryan, who had to figure out how to get to the hotel, drop our bags, and find his way back to Wrigley. In a city he knew nothing about. With little cash and no credit. But I had a job, and I had to do it, anxiety be damned.

"Sir?...Sir?" the media wrangler called out to me as I sat waiting in the Cubs dugout.

I snapped back into reality: "Yes! Sorry."

"Would you like to interview Mark Grace?" she asked.

"Absolutely," I quickly answered, as more than a decade of watching Grace's sweet batting-gloveless swing and defensive brilliance at first base rushed through my mind.

Before I knew it, Grace was sitting beside me and we were talking about Lynch, Sandberg, Sammy Sosa's epic home run duel with Mark McGwire from the summer before, Kerry Wood's arm injury, and the state of the 1999 Cubs.

"I trust in him," Grace said about Lynch. "Ed's pulled the trigger on some good deals for us. He's brought us some people in here that have helped us win immediately, and I respect him a lot for that."

Shortly after my interview with Grace ended, the 6-foot-6-inch Lynch walked up—dangerously close to scraping his head on the concrete ceiling of the dugout. He sat down, and we covered the things I'd discussed with Grace as well as Lynch's years as a Game-cock, his missing the Mets World Series run because of being traded to the Cubs, and more.

"Things worked out in the end," Lynch said of his June 1986 trade away from that year's ultimate World Champion. "I got a chance to pitch at Wrigley, in the greatest sports city in America. In retrospect, it was a very good thing for me."

As I made my way down the tunnel from the dugout to the Cubs clubhouse, I started to overthink what else I should have asked

Lynch. In the clubhouse I found second-year fireballer Kerry Wood, who was out for the season while recovering from Tommy John surgery. We discussed his 20-strikeout game, pitching in the 1998 playoffs, winning Rookie of the Year, having a former pitcher as a general manager, and carrying a pitching workload rumored to have led to his injury.

"I didn't get abused in the minor leagues," Wood told me, as we stood by his locker. "I think even at the major-league level, if we were up five or six runs, and I was going into the seventh or eighth, they would let the bullpen finish it out."

I now had pep in my step after my new best friend Kerry Wood and I finished talking. I walked from the clubhouse to the dugout and up its stairs to the field. Ten feet away, a gaggle of writers was speaking to All-Star outfielder Sammy Sosa, who'd spent the previous summer crushing 35 of his astounding 66 home runs out of Wrigley.

My stomach dropped when Bryan wasn't waiting in the stands behind the dugout as we'd planned. I badly wanted to interview Sammy, and began to walk in his direction. But my anxiety about Bryan took over, forcing me to take a right, quickly walk up the steps through the stands, back down the stairway that brought me into this house of worship, and out to the corner of Clark and Addison, to sit on the ground against Wrigley's outside wall to wait. And wait. And wait.

After about 30 more minutes sitting with my back against a wall near the ticket windows and worrying, I saw Bryan jump out of a cab and head toward me. A kind couple had given him money to catch a cab to Wrigley, so he'd finally made it. We went back into the park and found his seat. Then I headed to the press box to watch my first game at Wrigley alongside the Cubs and White Sox press corps.

With Bryan safe, my anxiety had receded and I was able to appreciate where I was and what I was doing—watching a Cubs game at Wrigley as a real reporter.

Two dreams coming true at once.

May 13, 2006

JOURNALISM HAD GIVEN me opportunities to meet many impressive and unforgettable people in the eight years since August of 1998, when I wrote my first story for *The State*, the daily newspaper in my hometown of Columbia.

Typically, today's dedication of a high school baseball field in southwest Michigan wouldn't have been a big deal. But the universe had one more surprise in store for me before my newspaper career—and my two-plus years as a reporter in the *South Bend Tribune*'s Michigan bureau—came to an end.

As they gathered on this Saturday morning to celebrate their field's renovation, the boys on the Niles High School baseball team slid their palms in and out of the legendary right hand of their teammate Asaad's father, who, along with the Detroit Tigers, had donated the funds needed to turn their old practice field into a regulation one.

Parkinson's disease didn't allow Muhammad Ali's body to act as it once did, but it hadn't changed his spirit. He said nothing as he shook hands with everyone in the gym, including me. But he looked deep into our eyes and smiled, conveying more than any words could deliver.

Later, as I crossed the Indiana-Michigan state line on my drive back to South Bend after writing my story, I reflected on my journalism career. I'd wanted to be a newspaper reporter since middle school, and for almost eight years, I had been. I wasn't at all ready to bid it farewell or prepared for what would happen when this massive part of my identity evaporated upon our move to Atlanta, after my wife Audrey[1] graduated from Notre Dame Law School.

During her commencement speech on May 21, one of Audrey's favorite law school professors (and future United States Supreme Court Justice) Amy Coney Barrett encouraged the Class of 2006 to give away 10 percent of their earnings to their church, to charitable causes, and to friends and acquaintances in need. "Your career and the money you earn shouldn't be directed just toward your own betterment but ought to be directed, in a tangible way, toward the common good," she told the future attorneys, who'd gathered with their friends and families to celebrate the culmination of their three years of grueling work.

Despite my private misgivings about my decision to walk away from my newspaper career, this section of Professor Barrett's speech made me feel like I was making the right decision: to leave journalism to serve the community in a new way. It also reminded me of my dad's suicide letter.

"I always went into career choices trying to decide how I could make the most money," my lawyer father had written. "I had to, since I didn't have any when I grew up. However, you don't have to make a choice on this criteria alone. I want you to do something that you enjoy and that will be beneficial to other people."

Even though my dad chose a career that earned him more than most, he'd still approached his work as a bankruptcy attorney with a heart for service. After he died, I'd heard stories about how he

---

1 Audrey's name has been changed out of respect for her wishes.

accepted payment from clients in vegetables they grew, and even in baseball cards that he then gave me.

In my heart, I wanted to make a greater impact in the community than I was making as a journalist, and I truly did want to focus on Involvement through News and Civics (which I'll refer to here as Inc), the nonprofit I'd founded in 2005. Audrey was supportive of my decision to focus full-time on this endeavor, even at the expense of a second income for our family.

But rolling up my sleeves to get Inc off the ground wasn't the whole story of why I was leaving journalism. Even though it had been my goal to write for a daily newspaper in a large city like Atlanta, the possibility of rejection—of failing to convince a paper that I was good enough to be hired—was too much for me to handle.

So, instead of engaging with the contacts I'd made at *The Atlanta Journal-Constitution* while Audrey was working as a summer associate in Atlanta in 2005, my fear of failure led me to never even apply for a position. Instead, I crafted the narrative for public consumption that I was starting a nonprofit and moving on from my career as a journalist. That story was 100 percent true, but I could have—and should have—been working on getting the nonprofit off the ground while continuing in my newspaper career.

Lonnie Ali gave her son's team a piece of advice that morning that I should have listened to for myself. She told them that all the donors could do was give them an *opportunity* to compete on a better field; *winning* was up to them.

"You have to seize the day," she emphasized.

But I was seized with fear, and make no mistake, the fear-based decision to leave the career I had built was all on my shoulders.

The Monday after her graduation, Audrey and I drove 705 miles from South Bend to Atlanta to start our new life. We were both filled with hope, but I was also filled with terror.

Yes, I wanted to serve the community in a new way. The problem was that I didn't know how to start a nonprofit, and I didn't know how to navigate a community without being a journalist.

I was completely lost, and it would take almost 18 months of fighting the worst depression and anxiety of my life for me to truly find my footing in Atlanta.

February 24, 2017

I NEVER KNEW HOW my dad's anniversary was going to hit me each year, nor did I ever really know how my anxiety or depression would affect me on any given day.

On this, the 21st anniversary of his suicide, a combination of grief and depression blindsided me, and I couldn't get out of bed.

Depression-related emotional paralysis wasn't rare for me. It happened often, manifesting itself on a spectrum from basic mental exhaustion to the physical inability to get out of bed. I'd choose to get lost in endless re-watches of *The Challenge* or *Survivor* or *Big Brother* or *Top Chef*. It was my attempt to forget my own pain and my inability to emotionally connect with others by investing in the characters and social dynamics of strategy-based reality competition shows.

As pathetic as it sounds, getting lost in the drama, romances, and friendships between real, but far-removed, people on the screen of my laptop or TV not only allowed me an escape, but reminded me that connection is possible. My investment in these people, and in the social and physical games in which they were competing, had helped me push through my suicidal ideas far more often than I'd liked to admit.

I'd spent countless days of my life trapped in this paralysis, but at least those days were usually lost in the comfort of my own bed, where no one was expecting anything from me in the first place.

On this particular day, however, I wasn't in my own bed in Atlanta, my home since 2006. I was in New York City—my happy place—at The New Yorker Hotel, across the street from Penn Station on 8th Avenue.

But mental illness doesn't care where we are, and is ready to wreak havoc on our minds, hearts, and souls regardless of our location or commitments to others.

Despite my anxiety and depression having been present in some fashion on all of my 15 prior trips to New York City between 1994 and now, today was different. This trip to remember my dad around the anniversary of his suicide was even more reflective, because when I returned to Atlanta, I'd only be the executive director of VOX Teen Communications for another week.

I'd announced six weeks earlier that, after four years there, I'd be resigning to launch my own consulting business, Five Points Civic Strategies.

I was hoping that at Five Points, I'd be able to deftly balance a mix of nonprofit and political clients. It would place me in the middle of a political world that, despite my being involved in it since late 2007, I hadn't yet realized was so unbearably toxic for me.

When I'd joined VOX as executive director in January 2013, it had legitimately been my dream job, allowing me to detach from politics to work with teen journalists—as I had been in high school for *The Viking Shield*—while leading an established and important Atlanta nonprofit.

Following my mid-2015 decision to divorce Audrey, my wife of 13 years, my insecurity and need to prove myself had become more and more present at VOX, and I'd unintentionally turned our fun, colorfully decorated newsroom into a toxic workplace for our adult staff. Though I'd tried to listen to the feedback given to me, I didn't know how to fix what I'd broken through my failed leadership.

I knew it was time for a change, and I was excited that my first hire at VOX, Susan, would deservedly be inheriting the executive director role.

Susan had joined VOX as our development director in May 2014, become our program director in September 2015, and our associate director in 2016. She could do all the things I could do as the nonprofit's day-to-day leader, but also so much more: she was able to engage and connect with our teens consistently while leading a healthy culture for our adult staff. She was the perfect leader for VOX.

In 2016, my drinking increased as my emotional stability frayed. At the same time, my focus on VOX lessened as I was pulled back toward politics to help my friend David win a seat in the Georgia House of Representatives. I hid from our adult staff and teens in plain sight. I wore my unprocessed pain and anxiety on my sleeve and face. I put up emotional walls (and even lashed out) instead of embracing vulnerability and allowing connection of any kind.

For the first time since I had joined VOX, I was getting paid for political campaign work again—as a side hustle. I thought I could do both, and maybe in a healthy mental state I could have, but I wasn't well. My emotional frailty had caused me to create unnecessary stress and drama both on the campaign and at VOX. I was inconsistent in my words and actions, and I felt like I was a bomb that could explode, thanks to the trigger of a misheard comment or misinterpreted suggestion from the adults around me.

In spite of my instability, our campaign team did excellent work to ensure David's election from his July 2016 runoff, and VOX had continued to be a safe, healthy place for our teens. But my issues and Jekyll & Hyde unpredictability had created stress and unneeded conflict with adults I cared about in both places, damaging relationships and putting more distance between myself and what I actually desired—connection and appreciation.

Instead of following through with the plans I'd made for today in New York, I was trapped in my bed and my mind, obsessing over failures, regrets, and the deep belief that I was walking a similar path to my dad's that would lead to my inevitable suicide.

I was supposed to introduce my friend Natalie to Bill's Place, the Harlem speakeasy where a teenaged Billie Holiday was discovered, to listen to some of the best jazz in the five boroughs—but I was literally unable to leave my bed.

Before my arrival at VOX, Natalie had been one of VOX's star storytellers when she was in high school. She'd created her own spoken-word poetry nonprofit, then interned with us at VOX while she was home from college during the summer of 2013. After she returned to Atlanta following her college graduation in 2015, we'd worked together to bring her nonprofit, Atlanta Word Works, into VOX, and then I'd hired her to run this exciting new program.

Natalie, one of the most talented storytellers I'd ever known, was now in grad school, studying Film at New York University. I'd been excited at the prospect of seeing her again, but my mental illness had other plans.

I told her I was sick, which wasn't exactly a lie, but it wasn't the full truth either. The fact was, I might as well have been in my bed in Atlanta, since all I was able to do was order pizza to my hotel room and stay glued to reality TV on my laptop until I mercifully slipped off to sleep to hide from my anxiety, depression, and suicidal thoughts.

Dreams seemed like the only place where I could connect with other people, inasmuch as my dream-based experiences always included others, and my anxiety and depression seemed to rarely appear in any form. Some people dream about grandiose things, but I tend to dream about having the kind of normal, healthy relationships with other human beings that in real life, I can't seem to ever get right.

I know that a large part of my failure in interpersonal relationships is my inability to get myself out of bed on days like this when connection with others is possible.

But I also know that if I choose to stay alive today, I'll have another chance tomorrow to fight my way out of bed, and out of the darkness that can overtake me in these moments. And then I'll have another chance to find the human connection that often eludes me.

December 2, 2009

A S W E E X I T E D our Delta flight from Atlanta to Reagan National, my iPhone powered back on and began to buzz with texts about last night.

Amir had lost in the runoff election, but he'd be back. The texts were congratulating me for the work our team had done to try and elect him to the Atlanta City Council. It was my first paid campaign job. I'd learned a ton and made lots of new friends and political allies.

But I wasn't taking a holiday break. Elena and I were heading to her hometown of Alexandria, Virginia, for a baby shower fundraiser with her friends and family. Less than three months earlier, after I'd been volunteering for her on the side during Amir's campaign, Elena had invited me to manage her campaign for a seat in the Georgia Legislature and shared her pregnancy news in the same conversation.

Elena, much like Amir, was a young attorney with a warm, inviting personality that put you at ease, a sharp mind, and a full commitment to public service. Both of them wanted to serve the voters and create progressive impact for the right reasons—not simply for the adulation, access, and accomplishment that come with being elected to political office when you're in your 30s.

Today was my first official day as a campaign manager. I'd be meeting Elena's parents and two sisters, spending a few days with them here in the DC area, and then flying to Minneapolis to join 34 up-and-coming progressive political operatives for Wellstone Action's week-long, intensive Advanced Campaign Management School (ACMS) program.

The time with Elena and her family was fun and productive, but before I knew it, I had landed in Minnesota. As I rode into town from the airport, I could have sworn this was the desolate ice world Hoth from *The Empire Strikes Back*, not just a normal, snow-blanketed, below-zero December night in Minneapolis.

Fortunately, I'd barely have to go outside since I was staying at the same hotel as the ACMS program, which complemented the crash course I'd received on Amir's campaign from our tough but extremely talented campaign manager, Howard, over the previous six months as we crisscrossed Atlanta's neighborhoods on foot while working to elect Amir.

A Wellstone Action alumnus himself, Howard had instilled in me the grassroots, direct-voter-contact philosophy that had elected Paul Wellstone to the US Senate in 1990. A true man of the people, Sen. Wellstone had served Minnesota until his death in a plane crash with his wife Sheila and six others on October 25, 2002. Wellstone Action had been founded in honor of Paul and Sheila to teach progressive organizing.

The intense but informal training I'd received through Howard's daily political insights and teachings during Amir's campaign was reinforced and broadened during the deeper ACMS training. I returned to Atlanta with the confidence, resources, and knowledge to build a campaign with Elena designed to defeat her incumbent Republican opponent on November 2, 2010.

On February 25, the day after the 14th anniversary of Dad's suicide, Elena's son Brooks was born. Less than three weeks later, we were sitting together at her kitchen table, interviewing Liz and Joe, who had traveled to Atlanta from Elena's hometown of Alexandria to pitch her on their direct mail and political consulting services. Their combined talent, razor-sharp political minds, storytelling prowess, and alignment on the vital role of the grassroots direct voter contact we were planning made them the perfect firm to elevate our team to the next level. We hired them that night, and I began working with them immediately.

The next week, Elena told me it was time to dig in and re-start her campaign. By March 29, we were working together daily again. By then, she'd already raised $100,000 with the help of call-time manager and Young Democrats of Atlanta friend Joshua, who had served as Amir's excellent finance director.

Our campaign plan called for Elena to knock on more than 10,000 doors, a number at which she didn't blink. By early May, she was in a daily walking routine to talk to her neighbors about what they cared about and needed from their state representative.

But before we set up our campaign office in Elena's basement with leftover, donated furniture from Amir's race, President Obama had signed the Affordable Care Act into law on March 23. This monumental legislation had created healthcare access for all—and the Tea Party movement.

As Obama Democrats, we were excited for and supportive of this historic legislation. The folks on the other side of the aisle were not so thrilled, and 2010 would prove to be an incredibly difficult year for Democrats because of the vitriol toward President Obama and the backlash against progressive policies that would send the Tea Party to Congress. But we were focused on Elena's race, and we knew if enough people could meet Elena in person and hear her vision, they would elect her to the Georgia House of Representatives on November 2.

As spring became summer, Elena's mornings were spent raising Brooks and campaign dollars, while her late afternoons and early evenings were set aside for walking her district to knock on doors and talk to voters. While she connected with voters, I earned the nickname "campaign manny" for doing everything from changing diapers, to executing campaign plans and managing the team, to bottle feeding the baby while coordinating mail with Liz and Joe.

We had a long way to go, but we had an inspiring and indefatigable candidate who was willing to put in the work on the phones and knocking on doors.

We also had a badass team that was fully committed to giving Elena everything she needed to thrive as a candidate: Briley, the ideal "candidate's spouse"; Leslie, coordinating volunteers, field, and outreach; Bess, leading fundraising and donor engagement; Carolyn, focused on Latinx engagement in the Buford Highway corridor; super-intern John, doing a little of everything; and Democratic House Caucus Director Don, supporting us daily with strategic counsel.

All we had to do now was win.

September 11, 2001

W<small>E WERE LIKE</small> kids on a playground at recess as we snuck into what was left of one of South Carolina's first mills.

We climbed the rubble. We breathed in the cool, crisp air. Sallie took pictures. Chris took notes. And I just took it all in.

It was one of those perfect moments. Beautiful scenery. Perfect weather. A great team. Actual journalism.

Everything seemed possible.

But the world was about to be blindsided.

On normal days, I would be at my desk by 9 a.m. in our two-person business writing department at the *Herald-Journal* in Spartanburg, South Carolina. But this morning, Chris, Sallie, and I had started working earlier than normal to drive to Pelham Mill, which sat about five miles south of the Greenville-Spartanburg International Airport (GSP), where, unexpectedly, we would later spend most of this Tuesday.

We'd arrived around 8 a.m. so that Sallie's lens could capture the mill in its early morning light. The visit and the shot were for a series Chris, our business editor, had conceived, called "The Unraveling of Textiles," documenting the crumbling textile manufacturing landscape across the Upstate, the South, and the country following the North American Free Trade Agreement, which had chipped away at blue collar lives and textile profit-and-loss statements since taking effect on January 1, 1994.

After our innocent frolicking about the mill's remains, we returned to Chris's Jeep Cherokee, where he found several missed calls on his phone from his girlfriend, Bridget, also a reporter at our paper. He called back and learned that something was happening in New York City.

A plane had hit the World Trade Center.

At that point, we knew little about what happened or what was about to happen. But as the business team for the paper, it was normally our job to cover the airport.

So, we headed to GSP to do our job. By the time we arrived, video of United Airlines Flight 175 hitting the south tower was playing on a loop at the airport bar as the patrons, like the entire country, watched 9/11 unfold live on television. This, we learned, was the second plane to hit the towers; at this point, there was no video of the first strike by American Airlines Flight 11, which had been hijacked and turned into a Boeing 767 missile carrying—and then ending—92 lives.

Just as she had at the mill, Sallie took photos. Chris and I observed and engaged with people milling around the airport in shock and watching the news. We were journalists covering the story—but we were also Americans experiencing the terror and the tragedy of what we saw transpiring on the TV screens.

At 9:45 a.m.—seven minutes after American Airlines Flight 77 crashed into the Pentagon—all airspace over the United States was shut down. Waiting travelers were officially stranded at GSP and, 14 minutes later, gasps and screams echoed in unison across the concourse as the south tower of the World Trade Center collapsed, live on network television.

Chris stayed in touch with our managing editor about our revised assignment, a reaction story from GSP that we would dictate over the phone for a special afternoon edition of the paper. We weren't yet writing live for the web, and social media as we now know it was still years away. We were closer to pre-internet newspaper days than we were to how we now consume news. Even with that in mind, an afternoon edition was virtually unheard of, but almost every paper in America created one that Tuesday. In massive bold type the *Herald-Journal*'s afternoon headline read:

U.S. ATTACKED

Beneath the headline and above the Associated Press photos of the second plane approaching the towers on the left and its explosion on the right, a subhead read: Hijacked Jets Level World Trade Center Towers, Third Plane Strikes Pentagon.

That day's terrorism killed almost 3,000 people.

We talked to dozens and dozens of people that day. Some were quoted in our joint-bylined stories in the afternoon edition and the next morning's paper. Most were simply conversations with other Americans, who were reacting to what we were seeing and hearing through their shock at what happened and their terror of what might happen next.

I drove back and forth to GSP that week, spending most of each day there because air travel didn't resume until late on September 13. People were stuck in Greenville—some stayed at the airport—so there were many stories to capture and share.

But I don't remember actually leaving the airport that Tuesday afternoon. It happened, of course, but my September 11 memories jump from the intensity of reporting at GSP to the darkness and isolation I felt that evening after returning home. Every channel was about the attacks. There were no baseball games, or *Friends* reruns, or canned escape of any sort from the reality of what had happened that morning, and what my anxiety told me might happen again at any moment.

Audrey was a 90-minute drive south, in the early days of her senior year at USC, so I was alone. She and I had been engaged for less than five months at that point; we were to be married in June 2002. At this time, she didn't even have a cell phone. In retrospect, it seems miraculous that we connected on her dorm room landline at all that day.

Everything was uncertain. I felt isolated and terrified. I didn't know then what an anxiety disorder was, or that mine had been growing inside me since middle school. But in the wake of that terrible Tuesday, as I watched the news nonstop, anxiety would envelop me that dark night in ways that I could not fathom. I felt helpless, scared, angry, and lost.

As an angsty 23-year-old who listened to lots of emo music, the blink-182 song "Anthem Part Two" was stuck in my CD player and my head for weeks after the attacks, constantly reminding me of the state of our world.

"Everything has fallen to pieces," the song began. "Earth is dying, help me Jesus."

In reality, I was alive and, in theory, I was safe. But the beginning of this song mirrored perfectly how terribly unprepared my mind was for living in this new world. That unpreparedness would fundamentally impact my rapidly devolving mental health.

June 11, 2016

I COULD SEE FREEDOM Tower (a.k.a. One World Trade Center) through the window and across New York Harbor, over the right shoulder of the life-sized bronze sculpture of the Tuskegee Airman being pierced from all angles by miniature bronze airplanes.

I assumed the statue's placement was by design.

Michael Richards used a mold of his own body in 1999 to create this sculpture, Tar Baby vs. St. Sebastian. The lore was that Richards foresaw his own death with this piece.

He spent the night of September 10, 2001, in his studio on the 92nd floor of the World Trade Center, where he'd earned a residency at the Lower Manhattan Cultural Council (LMCC) and lost his life the next morning.

Now, nearing the 15th anniversary of the terrorist attacks, the LMCC was spotlighting his work as part of its summer exhibition on Governor's Island, a mile south of Battery Park and only accessible from Manhattan by ferry.

I'd never been there before, so I arrived early before meeting my friend Hayley for a play on the island. She always found the most eclectic, memorable, and enjoyable experiences for us to share when I came to visit, which had become a several-time-a-year routine since March 2014.

We'd listened to dynamic jazz at Bill's Place, the Harlem speakeasy where a teenaged Billie Holiday was discovered in 1933. We'd watched Louis Malle's first film, *Elevator to the Gallows*, at Film Forum and marveled at Miles Davis's fully improvised jazz score. We'd ridden the Steeplechase at Coney Island. We'd laughed through *Night Train with Wyatt Cynac* at Littlefield. We'd explored every inch of the exhibit *Witness: Art and Civil Rights in the Sixties* at the Brooklyn Museum. And we'd eaten dozens of unforgettable meals: spicy, mouth-watering arepas at Arepa Lady in Jackson Heights; buttery, flaky croissants at Buvette in the West Village; and out-of-this-world pizza at Emily in Clinton Hill, to name just a few.

Hayley and I had met in 2009 in Atlanta while working together on Amir's first campaign. She too had lost her dad to suicide when she was a kid, and we'd connected around our shared trauma over a late-night meal at Majestic Diner. She was a kindred spirit and an irreplaceable friend.

Between Richards's poignant and eerie exhibit with lower Manhattan framed in the background, hundreds of people in 1920s-themed garb visiting the island for the annual Jazz Age Lawn Party, and the experience of the play we were about to see, it seemed like on this excursion, I'd gone through the looking glass in the best way imaginable.

Once Hayley arrived, we joyfully rode Citi Bikes around the island until it was time to walk to the 3:30 p.m. performance of Alexis Schaetzle's *Wanda, Daisy, & The Great Rapture*, a play neither of us knew much about. That was part of the fun. "Could be super weird and terrible," Hayley joked in her email suggesting we go to the play.

It turned out to be transcendent.

The play was presented at one of the yellow houses that lined Nolan Park on the northeast tip of the island. These homes reminded me of a two-story version of the ones at the Others' compound on

Lost. They'd once housed military officers, and they'd been re-envisioned for summer by arts organizations as exhibits, shops, and performance spaces.

Hayley and I leaned against the railing on the front porch of House 17 and caught up as we awaited instruction from members of the Brooklyn-based Exquisite Corpse Company. Minutes later, we were directed to move to the front yard so the play could begin on the porch where we were chatting.

Clearly, this was to be no typical play—in staging, story, and, ultimately, significance—and moments after we became the last members of the audience to gather in the yard, separated half-sisters Wanda and Daisy reunited on the house's front porch, whisking us away to fictional Crawley Island, off the coast of Myrtle Beach in my actual home state of South Carolina.

"It's been six months, do I even get a damn hug?" Daisy, 17, snips at her older half-sister, who we soon come to understand has been taking care of Daisy's father, Bud, who is only in his late 40s but is "deteriorating" from early-onset Alzheimer's.

Wanda, 20, works at the Piggly Wiggly to support their family, and wasn't expecting Daisy's return from New Horizons, a school for "troubled girls." Soon, Bud comes out of the house. Daisy runs to him and embraces her dad.

"Who are you? What are you doing in my yard?" he asks, staring at her. "Dad. It's me. Daisy. I'm here for Theresa Lee's funeral."

From here, we were ushered up the front staircase, across the porch, and into an empty living room to follow the action from beat-up, metal folding chairs.

We learned that Wanda's mom's funeral has already happened offstage. Her cause of death is then implied—transporting me back to the awful morning of February 24, 1996.

"People at the funeral were whispering about how Theresa Lee isn't gonna get into heaven on account of how she died," Daisy tells Wanda.

The drama and words dancing around me through the play's experiential staging seemed as if they were destined to lure me to *this* island on *this* day, as if I were a passenger on Oceanic Flight 815 when it crashed on September 22, 2004, during the pilot of *Lost*.

I had to catch my breath. South Carolina. Suicide.

Theresa Lee's spirit popped in and out of the play just like my dad has done in my dreams in the years since his suicide, making the discourse between her and Wanda a surreal experience for me.

I wished I could see and hear my dad too. And the parallels didn't stop there.

It's deeply spooky when an actor breathes life into words from a genius writer you've never met, giving an exact example of a concept that you've never said out loud but that has bounced around your mind for 20 years.

"It's our history," Theresa Lee says of their family's multiple suicides. "At a certain point, you go under water and you just can't come back up."

That palpable sense of drowning was exactly how I felt when I was paralyzed by depression and suicidal ideation. I could see the surface but couldn't reach it. Who was this writer, and how did our minds share this simple but personal metaphor?

Wanda, Daisy, & The Great Rapture was remarkably special to me from beginning to end.

Maybe it was unique because I'd never before experienced a story literally being told around me, rather than on an elevated stage. Maybe it was the masterful writing. Maybe it was incredible because of the connection I felt to these characters, to my dad, and to Hayley as we were transported a world away to the humidity and hallmarks of my South Carolina home.

The combination of Alexis Schaetzle's beautiful words, Kayla Catan's subtle but stellar performance as Wanda, and the immersive storytelling added up to a viscerally memorable experience that wouldn't soon leave my memory.

I've been moved and deeply affected—and even transformed—by many stories written by many storytellers and performed expertly by many actors on many New York stages, but this was different.

This was rapturous.

August 9, 2013

I'VE LOVED FILMS for as long as I can remember.

My first movie experiences were similar to most kids of the 1980s. Some nights, I enjoyed that immersive movie theater experience with friends or family. But on countless others, we'd go browse Blockbuster for an hour before renting our favorites again and again—unless we'd already taped them off HBO or, in rare cases, had actually bought our own VHS copy. *The Goonies* joined *Grease*, *Back to the Future*, the original *Star Wars* trilogy, and *Top Gun* on the short list of movies we owned and watched over and over. I still quote them.

It was a misty, gloomy day in Astoria, Oregon, as my wife Audrey and I parked a few yards away from the steep driveway that led to the large, two-story white house with the wraparound porch at the top of the hill. Gone was the Rube Goldberg-esque device Mikey designed to open the gate after forcing Chunk to do the Truffle Shuffle, but it was unmistakable: this was *the* house from *The Goonies*.

We only stayed for a few minutes so as not to disturb the homeowners, but it was fun to show Audrey this piece of my childhood. Less than an hour before, we'd visited the Oregon Film Museum, which is located in the "County Jail" building from the same movie. If you go there, you'll know you've arrived because parked out front of the gray, two-story building sits the Fratellis' black Jeep Cherokee with "bullet holes the size of matzo balls," as per Chunk's description in the film.

Audrey was always such a great sport about my desire to seek out film locations like these. A few days earlier, we'd gone on a three-hour film tour of San Francisco—an excellent way to see the city. Later that same day, on our way to Seattle from Astoria, we'd visited Stadium High School in Tacoma, where *10 Things I Hate About You* was filmed, and then The Coryell Court apartment building on East Thomas Avenue in Seattle, where *Singles* had been shot.

In a Seattle surprise the next evening, we learned about (and then attended) an outdoor screening of *The Goonies* on the grass beside the Museum of History and Industry, with the Space Needle in the distance, perfectly framed behind the left side of the inflatable screen.

I'd bought *The Goonies* on DVD not long after I'd acquired my first DVD player in 2001. This had been my main splurge after I started my first full-time, post-graduate newspaper job in Spartanburg at the *Herald-Journal*. DVDs were designed to be collected, and my anxiety loved manifesting itself in building collections, whether baseball cards or cookbooks or movies.

My movie tastes have expanded over the years, as has my far-too-large DVD/Blu-Ray collection of almost 5,000 movies. I'm now as excited to experience the storytelling in Claire Denis's *Beau Travail* or Akira Kurosawa's *Seven Samurai*; in Spike Lee's *Do the Right Thing* or Ingmar Bergman's *Persona;* or in Chantal Akerman's *Jeanne Dielman, 23, quai du Commerce, 1080 Bruxelles,* as I am to watch the American popcorn flicks on which I was raised.

To me, film is a time machine. It can whisk us away to every corner of the world and back and forth through time. Its images connect us to humanity and inhumanity at 24 frames per second in order to teach us how to embrace the former and avoid the latter.

In 2003, after Audrey started law school, I needed something to do in my free time, since she had very little of it to spare. I set myself the goal of watching the entire American Film Institute Top 100 list along with the many Best Picture winners that I hadn't yet seen. I already loved quite a few—*Star Wars, Pulp Fiction, Taxi Driver, The Apartment, The Godfather*—but there were so many more that I truly needed to experience. How had I not seen *On the Waterfront,* or *Lawrence of Arabia, Casablanca, Vertigo,* or *City Lights*?

So, I decided to purchase and watch every film that I needed to expand my horizons—and my collection. A few weren't available and wouldn't be until high-definition Blu-Ray discs began to debut in 2007. While hunting for hard-to-find yet reasonably priced copies of *The Third Man* and *Rebecca,* I made the life-changing discovery of The Criterion Collection, a treasure trove of essential films from across the world.

I decided that once I had completed the AFI 100 and Best Picture Winners, I would begin to dig into the films of The Criterion Collection, which has been called "film school in a box." Now, I trust them to introduce me monthly to artists I might never discover, like Miranda July or Charles Burnett or Věra Chytilová or Marlon Riggs or Céline Sciamma.

I can honestly say that my passion for immersing myself in cinema allows me to broaden my perspective and deepen my humanity. But it's not an entirely healthy passion, because experiencing films only at home—especially through collecting—exacerbates my isolation and disconnection from others. In a 2012 *Psychology Today* article, Susan Krauss Whitbourne said that collectors like me "may also begin to feel guilty and become socially isolated as they disappear more and more into their collections." I've found this to be definitely true for me because my anxiety disorder and my film collection have grown in tandem.

"For some, the satisfaction comes from experimenting with arranging, re-arranging, and classifying parts of a-big-world-out-there, which can serve as a means of control to elicit a comfort zone in one's life, e.g., calming fears, erasing insecurity," Mark McKinley wrote in 2007 in *The National Psychologist* about the psychology of collecting.

Like so many addictions, it's all about excess versus balance.

I'm grateful to continue to expand my world through cinema, as the introvert in me will always need to detach and recharge. I just have to remember to go outside and experience the world as well, even if it is to see a movie in a park.

May 30, 2016

A FEW DAYS AGO, my coworker Susan had posed a question to me for which I had no answer. "What brings you joy?" she asked, as I sat across from her desk in the VOX newsroom.

I'd hired Susan as our development director a little more than two years earlier, and it was the best decision I ever made during my years at VOX.

I said then that I'd think about her question. Now, Wrigley Field had answered it for me.

While Audrey was in law school from 2003 to 2006 and we lived in South Bend, I'd gone several times a season, happily traveling 100 miles each way. Today, I was back at this hallowed place for the first time in a decade.

The game was over. The Cubs had just completed a 2–0 Memorial Day shutout of the Los Angeles Dodgers under clear blue afternoon skies, with the temperature in the mid-70s and a slight breeze blowing off the lake. It was completely perfect, and I felt and absorbed every sensation as I sat along the third base line, about 20 rows from the field.

This was joy.

As Wrigley began to empty out, I stayed an extra 25 minutes, just to revel in this newfound feeling and reflect on so many Cubs memories I'd acquired throughout my life.

I remembered all the afternoons watching Cubs games on WGN after school. I remembered the 1990 All-Star game at Wrigley, and the worst Home Run Derby *ever* the day before, with the wind roaring in off the lake, limiting the field of eight sluggers to only five home runs—in total! Ryne Sandberg hit three, walking away with the trophy and the title.

I remembered my first trip to New York, in June 1994, when I'd been stunned to learn about Sandberg's surprise retirement. Right behind that came the memory of his return to the Cubs on April 1, 1996—which he'd announced on March 3, bringing me a moment of joy a week after Dad's suicide. And I remembered writing my story on Ed Lynch and skipping a Sammy Sosa interview to sit out front of Wrigley until Bryan finally arrived from his 17th birthday, lost-in-Chicago adventure in June 1999.

I remembered sitting in a dorm room on the second floor of the Sigma Chi hall at USC on September 28, 1998, biting my nails to the quick watching the Cubs beat the Giants 5–3 in a one-game Wild Card tiebreaker, while simultaneously awaiting the (ultimately affirmative) results of the brothers' vote on allowing me to affiliate with their chapter after transferring to USC from Alabama.

I remembered spending the evening of October 5, 2003, at the Buffalo Wild Wings in Goshen, Indiana, while on assignment for *The Elkhart Truth*, which had given me my first newspaper job after we moved to South Bend. The Cubs beat the Braves to win their first postseason series since 1908 that night, before heartbreak returned in the 2003 National League Championship Series when the Cubs were four outs away from beating the Marlins to go to the World Series, but fell apart in the eighth inning of Game 6 and then lost Game 7 as well.

I remembered May 2004, when Audrey and I took in one of the coldest games I'd ever attended at Wrigley, along with my cousin Gina and her husband Josh, who were in Chicago for a conference.

Gina wanted hot chocolate to warm up, but Josh misheard and hilariously brought her a hot dog instead.

I remembered sitting on the floor of our South Bend apartment with our yellow lab, Sandberg, on July 31, 2005, watching his namesake make his Hall of Fame induction speech in Cooperstown. And I remembered being at Wrigley on August 28, 2005, for Sandberg Day, as they retired the new Hall of Famer's Number 23, raising a flag embossed with his last name and number to forever fly from the right field foul pole, under Billy Williams's Number 26.

I remembered watching games from the legendary bleachers, the press box, and a dozen other places in Wrigley during our years living in the Midwest. And I remembered watching the Cubs play on the road in San Diego, Los Angeles, and of course, at Turner Field in Atlanta—especially on June 8, 2007, when left fielder Alfonso Soriano crushed three homers to help destroy the Braves 9–1.

So many games. So much fun. More than enough heartbreak for a devoted fan. So much *joy* that I'd forgotten. But now I was remembering, and realizing the things that truly brought me joy. Baseball. Dogs. Travel. Reflection. Family.

Five months later, on November 2, the Cubs would end the 2016 season by doing the unimaginable. In Game 7, they beat the Indians 8–7 in 10 innings in Cleveland to win the World Series after a 108-year championship drought, delivering infinite joy to me and to millions of other Cubs fans.

February 16, 2000

I HIT SEND ON the email at exactly 6 p.m.

She was the first in my family to learn about this story, not over the phone or in person, but in writing—and preceded by my byline.

The email went to vera29016@aol.com.

In the late 1970s, her friends called her V. But when I was learning to talk, I couldn't exactly say Vee.

So, she became Bee, and as the first of four grandchildren that she adored, toddler Jeffrey (I became Jeff when we started writing in cursive) had the true honor of bestowing upon her the name she'd be known by for the rest of her life.

Vera Riley loved writing, sports, and her family.

Bee's next America Online log-on would trigger the robotic "You've got mail" greeting, and she'd find an email that checked all three of those boxes.

The story I shared was set to run Friday in *The Gamecock*, USC's student newspaper, which—in addition to my work at *The State*—I wrote for on and off while I was attending USC, from August 1998 through my December 2000 graduation.

Here's my column as it appeared in *The Gamecock* on February 18, 2000, and in my email to Bee.

BY JEFF ROMIG, SPORTS EDITOR

I've covered a lot of high school basketball games during my tenure as a freelance reporter for *The State*.

I'll usually get a call from my boss, Fred, on Mondays letting me know what assignments he wants me to cover that week. This week was no different.

Fred called on Monday asking me to cover Tuesday night's match-up between the Hammond and Cardinal Newman boys' basketball teams.

If Hammond won, they would clinch their region with an undefeated region record.

If Cardinal Newman won, the two teams would stand tied with one game left for each team to play.

There was one thing different about this particular game though. Fred asked me to do a feature story on one of Hammond's players while I was there. This was a good thing because bills were overdue and two stories means twice the pay. But what I would eventually get from this experience would be much more valuable than any monetary sum.

Hammond pulled out a 60–52 win after a fourth quarter spurt. All was well for the Skyhawks as they captured their third consecutive regional title. When the game ended, I waited outside Hammond's locker room for Jimmy Braddock, the Skyhawks' head coach, to reappear after his post-game talk with his players.

We talked about the game. We talked about the region championship. We talked about his star center, Zeb, and then about his small forward, Robert, whom I was to do the feature story on. When I finished talking to Braddock, he introduced me to Robert. We then chatted for a few minutes about basketball, his torn ACL, and his upcoming baseball season. After several minutes had passed, I felt like I had sufficient information between Robert and his coach to write a solid feature.

I turned off my tape recorder and left the gym to write my game story. When I finished writing from my house, I was going to go ahead and write my feature on Robert while the information was fresh in my mind. But I procrastinated.

Since my deadline was Friday, there was no need to write another story at 11:30 p.m.

On Wednesday, I would go about my day as I normally would. I made a to-do list and carried out everything before I would return home. Everything except for one thing—I needed to write my story on Robert. It would be the first thing I would do when I got home. I would make it my top priority after I checked my messages and returned my calls.

I discarded the first two messages and jotted down whom I needed to call before I came to the third message—from Robert's father, Ron. He wanted to let me know that he had some additional information about Robert that I might be interested in. The information he intended to give me would add to my story, but what he didn't know was that the information that came up in conversation would add tremendously to my life.

Ron's an attorney in Columbia. I knew that thanks to Caller ID, but then he mentioned that he went to USC for law school after I told him that I was a student. I proceeded to tell him that my father attended law school at USC as well.

The obvious question followed: "Who is your father?"

"He died four years ago," I replied. "His name was Steven Romig." His response was unlike anything I could have ever expected. "I was going to ask," Ron said. "I worked with your father on many occasions. We were close business associates. I am in bankruptcy, as you know he was."

Of course, I knew. But I didn't know that my late father and Ron used to give each other work when the other was too busy. I also didn't know his lofty opinion of my dad.

"Your father was one of the nicest people I ever worked for," Ron said. "One of the smartest too. Your father was a brilliant man."

I was stunned. Not that I didn't believe these things myself, but to have someone you've never spoken to speak such accolades about your father out of nowhere was quite overwhelming. My father passed away on February 24, 1996—four years ago next week—but for a brief moment, he was alive again.

Ron's last words to me were: "It was a privilege to get to speak with Steve Romig's son."

No, Ron, it was a privilege to speak to you. Thank you for bringing my father back to life, if only for five minutes.

February 24, 2016

I T WAS ALMOST 11 a.m. in Paris. I was the first in my immediate family to observe the 20th anniversary of Dad's suicide, because Mom and Bryan were in America, still sleeping in a time zone where the clock read 6 a.m.

I had planned my first solo European vacation with the explicit goal to observe this day with adventure and fearlessness, rather than with the pain and grief that had accompanied the majority of the 19 prior anniversaries.

I was about to begin the second leg of this journey. The first leg was to Paris. For the past few days, I had enjoyed navigating the City of Light from my Airbnb on the Rue du Roule in the 1st arrondissement. I'd been to the Eiffel Tower and the Louvre. I'd walked along the Champs-Élysées toward the Arc de Triomphe, where I could almost hear the echoes of Jean Seberg's cooing voice as she peddled the *New York Herald-Tribune* in Jean-Luc Godard's *À bout de soufflé* (*Breathless*), one of my favorite films.

I'd sat on a bench near the banks of the Seine to read, write, and take in the real-life experience of Paris, comparing it to the black-and-white world I'd embraced through stories on screen from my favorite French directors: Jean Renoir, Jean-Pierre Melville, Francois Truffaut, Agnes Varda, and the aforementioned Godard.

I'd successfully used my limited French to order delectable pastries at pâtisseries and cafés. And I'd found an expat bar run by an American, where I could drink bourbon and have much-needed conversations and connections in English.

But I'd planned the vacation so that today would provide the journey's signature moment.

I would travel by train to Brussels, and then by car to Krinkelt, a tiny village in Belgium, about four miles from the western border of a desolate stretch of Dad's home country, Germany. I wanted to be in Belgium as part of today's anniversary observation, but also to focus on Papa, my maternal grandfather.

On December 17, 1944, Clyde Riley was 22, a soldier in the 99th Infantry Division of the United States Army, fighting in the Battle of Elsenborn Ridge. The Germans planned to use two key routes through the area to seize Antwerp. Hitler designed this attack to "surround and destroy" British and American forces, according to *The Ardennes: Battle of the Bulge,* written by Hugh M. Cole in 1965.

On December 16, 1944, at 5:30 a.m., in bitter cold temperatures, the Germans had launched their final major offensive campaign on the Western Front, inflicting 90 minutes of destruction across 80 miles of the Ardennes that were simultaneously being blanketed by a major snowstorm.

Capturing the twin villages of Rocherath and Krinkelt, east of Elsenborn Ridge, was essential to Hitler's plan.

Papa's 99th Infantry stood in the way. Because they were so young (20 years old, on average) and hadn't seen combat yet, his division was dubbed the Battle Babies. But how could 83,000 fresh, untested soldiers stop 200,000 Germans?

Ultimately, the area from Elsenborn Ridge to Monschau would be the only portion of the American front during the Battle of the Bulge where the Germans failed to advance. "Outnumbered five-to-one, the soldiers of the 99th inflicted casualties in the ratio of eighteen-to-one. The division lost more than one in five men, including

465 killed and 2,524 evacuated with wounds, injuries, fatigue, or trench foot," Rob Dean wrote in *Why the Bulge Didn't Break*.

During the fighting, Papa was separated from his unit and formally declared Missing in Action.

In notes for an unpublished memoir, Papa later shared his experience with death. His first brush had been when he was 17, losing his mother, Jesse, to a brain tumor less than three years before his time on the Belgian battlefield, where death was everywhere.

"There was constant awareness it could come to me at any moment," he wrote. "I can't even now know how I escaped. There were times when bullets seemed as raindrops around me, yet I remained dry, unhit. It is still a mystery."

To evade capture and death, Papa had hidden and fought to stay alive, eluding German soldiers in the southern tip of the Hürtgen Forest. Ultimately, the enemies that would take him down were the snow and ice surrounding his frozen feet.

He didn't remember collapsing or being rescued, but when he awoke, he was in an Army hospital, being treated for frostbite on his feet that would remain a constant, damaged trigger of the remembered horrors of war until his death, 70 years later.

Today, there is a monument in Krinkelt to the Battle Babies. About two years before my trip, my cousin Gina and her family had visited it in January 2014 while spending a month in Brussels. Papa had told Gina about the monument and said he'd love to see it.

"We had a free weekend, so we hired a car and drove, not knowing what we would see there," Gina said later. "We had not spent much time in Europe before, so our expectations were quite different from the reality!"

They'd planned to drive to the village of Krinkelt, eat lunch at a restaurant, ask for directions to the monument, and possibly spend the weekend exploring. But Krinkelt is tiny.

"We did not see a single person as we arrived," she said. "We weren't sure how we were going to find the monument since there were no people, and any signs we did see were only in German or French."

But, as they parked, they saw a giant American flag flying across the road, over the monument to the Battle Babies of the 99th. They stayed there for a while, taking pictures for Papa, and documenting its engraved words: "This monument stands in honor of members of the 99th Infantry Division and attached units who gallantly served and those who died for freedom and in the name of liberty during World War II in Europe. It is a memorial commemorating their service to mankind."

Additionally, there was a sign beside the monument that read: "May God help you to understand what the fighting here and in the area was like, for there was such a difference between those who suffered and those who observed the suffering from afar."

For Gina, Krinkelt was quiet and calm, but she was able to experience one element of what Papa had gone through in 1944: "Everything was covered in snow," she said. "I imagined it looked similar to what he saw."

She emailed the pictures they'd taken back to South Carolina for Papa to see. "He immediately recognized one of the houses where he had hidden out during some of the fighting," Gina had told me. "He was amazed at how similar it all still looked."

Now, on this cold, February day, it would be my turn to experience the small village that had had such a huge impact on the world, and on our family.

It had been little more than 80 minutes on the Thalys train from the Paris Nord station when I arrived at Bruxelles Midi. All that was left to do was find the Avis counter and get the rental car I'd reserved in January, when I'd decided to visit Krinkelt.

I'd envisioned that the two-hour drive across the Belgian countryside would be a great time to reflect on Dad and Papa (who had passed away at 92 in July 2014) before I spent a little time at the monument and in the sparsely populated village. Then I'd turn around and drive two hours back to Brussels, treat myself to a Belgian waffle, and catch my 8:38 p.m. return train to Paris.

I found the Avis window, handed the clerk my printed reservation and my passport, and waited to receive my keys so I could hit the road.

But I wasn't meant to visit Krinkelt that day.

Despite having my passport and my reservation documents, Avis also required my driver's license in order to permit me to drive away in the Volkswagen Polo reserved under my name.

My heart sank.

I hadn't needed my license in Paris because I had my passport, so I had taken it out of my wallet. It was back in my hotel room. And soon, I would be too, because sadly, there wasn't enough time left today to retrieve it and return, with the way the train schedule fell; and tomorrow, I was flying home.

I was heartbroken, but calm. It wasn't the end of the world. It was a day intended for perspective and reflection, and it remained exactly that as I watched the countryside of Belgium and France pass by my train window on the way back to Paris.

I thought about the sacrifices of Papa, of the brothers-in-arms he fought alongside, and of the people in so many villages like Krinkelt that had to be rebuilt in the years after the war.

I thought about Gina giving Papa the gift of those pictures; she was able to capture and share with him images of this place, which he'd thought he'd never again see with his own eyes.

I thought about the possibility of coming back sometime to try and make it to Krinkelt, and what that future day might feel like, when I'd be able to read the Battle Babies monument with my own eyes.

And I thought about my dad, and that life-changing day 20 years earlier, when I'd first read the final paragraph of his suicide letter.

"Life can be fun," he'd written. "Without money worries, you can make intelligent choices. I pray that you will make them. I look forward to seeing you again in heaven, but I will be looking over you through the balance of your life here on earth. Love always, Dad."

January 6, 2002

It was Bee's 73rd birthday, but the journal that her daughters, Sandra and Pam, gave her wasn't to be filled with just any writing. It was to be inscribed with memories and revelations, original poems, and Bible verses as she fully embraced a request made by her oldest grandson.

A few days earlier, she had inquired of me what I wanted for my 24th birthday, which falls a month plus one day after hers. I'd asked Bee—whose writing talent I'd inherited—to fill a journal with thoughts and memories about my dad.

Starting on the evening of her own birthday, she filled all 65 pages of the spiral-bound journal with what she called "random remembrances, entwined experiences, and joyful journeys with Steve."

Throughout my life, Bee had always been the most consistently positive person I'd ever known. But in these writings about her son-in-law and "best friend," I could feel her pain and sadness.

On page four, she wrote about their final chat.

"The last conversation I had with Steve was on the telephone," she wrote in her beautiful cursive. "I had seen the movie *Sense and Sensibility* and suggested he might like it. We discussed its principles and philosophies. He concluded: 'I'll have to put that one on my list.' He never got to see it. Time ran out for him."

She wrote that Steve was a man of few words. "But what he said, you understood and remembered," she underlined for emphasis. And she told a story that happened when I was a teen, but of which I had no memory: Bee was staying at our house while Papa was enduring one of his many hospital stays throughout the 1990s for the ongoing heart problems that had followed his 1989 quadruple bypass surgery. After dinner, she told Dad she liked our new microwave, adding that theirs had burned out and was beyond repair.

"Steve looked at Bryan and said, 'Let's go get Papa and Bee a new microwave oven like ours,'" she wrote. "Away they went to Best Buy. Before Clyde got out of the hospital, Steve went to our house and had the oven installed and working when we returned home. It's just one of those things that was little to Steve, but mighty big to us!"

Bee had met my dad in an English class at Augusta College after she'd gone back to school in the late 1960s. They'd studied together in the Augusta College cafeteria, and Bee and my dad had ultimately received their bachelor's degrees together in 1971. At some point, Bee had also introduced him to her older daughter, Sandra, who later became my mom.

She'd had a front-row seat to his mind for almost 30 years—for longer than anyone in our family.

"He could read a book in the evening, and tell you all about it when you asked," she remembered. "His superb comprehension came into play and was a great asset in the legal areas of his life. He had an ability to focus without wavering. His intelligence was evident and a mighty, mighty strength to him."

One day when they were studying in the cafeteria, former State Sen. Jimmy Carter, who was running to be Georgia's governor, stopped by their table, spoke to them for a few minutes, shook their hands, and went on to talk to more students. "I voted for him when he ran for president of the US, and he won," Bee wrote of President Carter. "I don't know who Steve voted for (in 1976) because that was his 'classified' information."

I could feel her smiling as she wrote that sentence, implying my dad's caginess about so many things in his head. But it was my dad's smile that was seared into her memory, along with those of so many of his friends after his death.

"Steve smiled more than he verbalized his innermost feelings," she remembered. "I never knew him without a smile. It always spoke in giving worlds of information."

I really don't remember much of my dad's funeral, which was held three days after his suicide. I remember talking to my middle school baseball buddies, Johnny and Fish, in the reception hall. I remember my sweet friend, Jamie, as she gave me a kiss on the cheek, and a hug as I ran into her on my way into the church. I remember Bryan sobbing. And I remember taking a rose off my dad's casket at the cemetery to keep forever. But that's about it. Those days are a blur.

On June 6, 1996, the Richland County Bar Association had held a memorial service for Dad. I hadn't attended, because I was working one of my first shifts as a server at Villa Tronco, but Bee had taken notes and shared them with me in her journal, quoting what others said about Dad, without attribution.

"He is remembered and revered."

"He was known as the best bankruptcy lawyer in the state."

"He was the epitome of a gentleman."

"When Steve died, I lost one of the best friends I ever had," she confided in the journal. "He knew. I told him so. I'm a better person because I walked and talked with Steve in a reciprocal relationship."

After he died, she'd written her perception of his death as an original poem, and reproduced it in this journal for me:

> *I am devastated but not*
> *destroyed,*
> *Disillusioned but not*
> *dysfunctional.*

I understand better how an
airplane
Can soar through the skies
with such dignity and beauty,
Crash and be in total
disarray within a few blinks
of the eye.

Steve was that way.
He humbly soared to the heights
of his profession
With all the acclaim due him
But in a twinkle he was
dead at the age of 47.

I came home to Columbia from Spartanburg the weekend after my 24th birthday to stay with my mom and celebrate with family and friends. When I returned home, I read my gift from Bee until I was out of pages and tears.

This was a moment in which words were absolutely my Kryptonite. I was in no way emotionally prepared to absorb Bee's insights and stories about Dad all at once.

My fear and anxiety had been accelerating since the days following the September 11th terrorist attacks five months before, and had begun to create physical problems for me throughout the fall and early winter.

Chills.

Nausea.

Racing heart.

Profuse sweating.

Breathing problems.

My symptoms were swirling around me. At first, they hit me one at a time, in isolation from each other, but with enough force for me to know something was changing. I was making fear-based decisions, like breaking my lease early to move to a new apartment, thinking a change of scenery would quell my accelerating and unstoppable anxiety.

The experience of consuming Bee's writing and, in the process, reliving Dad's suicide, had truly wrecked me. When I returned to Spartanburg after my birthday and the shock of reading the journal, my symptoms began to occur more frequently, and no longer in isolation.

They started to attack late at night, when I was too scared to inconvenience anyone by asking for help. I was terrified. Was I dying? Was I having a heart attack? Why wouldn't it stop? Who would take me to the ER? Should I call 911?

I felt like the walls were closing in on me. And even after the physical symptoms subsided, all it took was remembering the feeling of them to trigger another attack. This caused sleepless nights and affected everything in my life until I walked into my managing editor's office at the *Herald-Journal* one morning in March 2002 to admit that I needed help.

He supported my decision to take time off to go back to Columbia, see a psychiatrist, and investigate treatments for what I soon learned was panic disorder. Panic disorder leads to sudden and repeated fear-based attacks in which, even though there is no danger, the victim experiences an intense physical reaction to the fear of impending disaster or losing control.

I would soon receive a diagnosis of generalized anxiety, panic disorder, and clinical depression, and my first prescription for medication designed to re-balance the chemicals in my broken brain.

Initially, reading my grandmother's memories of my dad had crushed me. But information is power, and not only had I received an irreplaceable, cherished journal full of my grandmother's words, wisdom, and writing, it led me to the gift of my diagnoses.

Without a diagnosis, medicine, or asking for help, Dad broke in a way that wasn't fixable.

But for me, seeking treatment and then working daily to manage my diseases ultimately helped me find a way to deviate from his path, even though it wouldn't happen for another 15 years.

December 5, 2017

IT WAS JUST before noon. I passed a handful of strangers smoking cigarettes and turned right to walk down the four steep, cracked, concrete steps and through the metal door into the Alcoholics Anonymous meeting, which was taking place in the basement of The Church of Our Savior in Atlanta.

I kept my eyes on my feet the whole time as I walked through the room, and dropped into a black, cushioned metal chair on the right side of the gathering as fast as I could. I wouldn't speak for the next hour, and I'd leave without talking to anyone. I didn't know if I'd ever be back.

I thought my life was in free fall. And I certainly didn't think that this room, the meeting, and the people I'd ultimately connect with there would save my life. But for one hour each day, six days a week, they would.

For the city of Atlanta, it was Election Day to determine the winners of runoff contests from Nov. 7. But for me, today was Day Three of sobriety. I'd been to a different AA meeting each of those three days as I tried to find my footing in this new, sober life.

A month earlier, I'd helped my dear friend Amir win a seat on the Atlanta City Council. Up to a week ago, I'd been a senior adviser to more than half a dozen Atlanta Democrats through Five Points

Civic Strategies, the consultancy I'd started earlier in the year. Today, I was supposed to have been helping to elect the new mayor of Atlanta and a freshman state senator, both of whom were in run-off elections. But the week before, I'd quit—I'd quit everything, except for my actual life. All that had happened before seemed like a lifetime ago.

On another timeline, today could have easily been my final day on earth, because win or lose, my guaranteed binge drinking and probable drunk driving would have ensued, with potentially fatal consequences.

But instead, I was here at AA, listening to a woman open the meeting with the AA preamble: "Alcoholics Anonymous is a fellowship of men and women who share their experience, strength, and hope with each other that they may solve their common problem and help others to recover from alcoholism. The only requirement for AA membership is a desire to stop drinking. There are no dues or fees for AA membership; we are self-supporting through our own contributions. AA is not allied with any sect, denomination, politics, organization, or institution; does not wish to engage in any controversy, neither endorses nor opposes any causes. Our primary purpose is to stay sober and help other alcoholics to achieve sobriety."

She then turned the meeting over to the group for discussion and shares. I was far too scared to speak, but I knew I belonged in AA. I'd used to be able to easily stop after a couple of bourbons, taken as an antidote to counteract the effects of my social anxiety. I didn't drink all the time, or even at home much. But now, when I drank, I couldn't stop at a couple, and the shame I felt traced back to things I did and mistakes I made while drunk.

That wasn't who I wanted to be. So, the weekend before, I'd driven to Charlotte, North Carolina, to get away from Atlanta and talk to Jason, my college roommate, about how my drinking had changed over the past few years.

Jason and I had gone to high school together. He'd been two years behind me and best friends with my girlfriend, whom I had begun dating only two weeks after Dad's suicide. In 1998, I'd moved back to Columbia from Tuscaloosa to transfer home to USC. I'd quickly reconnected with Jason there. We'd ultimately become roommates—and I'd become a first-hand witness to his alcoholism.

In June 2001, Jason and I had sat on a boat docked in a Lake Murray cove near Columbia. He'd confided to me that he was an alcoholic and was seeking help through AA. In the ensuing 16-plus years, he'd been the co-best man in my 2002 wedding, alongside my brother. We'd lived in distant cities from each other in the Midwest and South. Then he lived in Atlanta for a bit. Now, he's married, a lawyer, and a father, with more than 16 years of consecutive sobriety. For almost 20 years, our friendship had ebbed and flowed through our individual journeys, but it has been that rare connection that will always be there despite our separate post-college lives.

Two weeks ago, after the most explicit suicidal planning I'd ever experienced—choosing and sharpening a knife and filling a bathtub with water—I'd called Jason and shamefully confessed that alcohol was destroying me, leaving out any mention the life-and-death nature of my despair.

He'd immediately invited me to come to Charlotte so we could talk in person. After I arrived, he'd handed me his copy of one of the most important books I'll ever read. He'd opened the blue hardback, circled sections for me to read that night, and then told me we needed to stop hanging out so I could start reading. "There's a meeting down the street at nine tomorrow morning," he'd told me. "After you read what I circled, we can go, if *you* decide you want to go."

I'd opened the instruction manual for life entitled *Alcoholics Anonymous*—eponymous with the name of its group meetings—and gotten to work, reading everything Jason circled, and more. I'd discovered that there was far more to relate to in what I was reading than was unrelatable.

Because of my need to be in control and my deep fear of social situations, I didn't drink in high school. Well, I'd had drinks, but I consciously didn't *drink*. After my dad's suicide, I'd codified that decision, pledging to not deal with my trauma and grief by drinking or doing drugs. For more than four years, I'd experienced college and grief without substances. Looking back, I was just scared. Scared of connecting with people. Scared of losing control. Scared of everything, pretty much.

Had I known that alcohol could completely eliminate these fears and anxieties, even for a brief time, maybe things would have been become far worse, far sooner.

In July 2000, I'd started my first romantic relationship since I'd moved home, and eased into drinking with a screwdriver that my future wife, Audrey, made me after one Gamecocks' football game. That was my drinking modus operandi for 14 years. Liquor drinks, but just a couple at a time. No beer. Never drinking past a buzz. Controlled.

But things changed in 2014. Papa, my grandfather and hero, died that summer. My meds were wrong and not working. My 12-year marriage to Audrey was crumbling.

I was extremely lost. So I drank more.

I'd rarely drink at home—and I'd never used any unprescribed drugs—but socially, which even at my worst was only a handful of nights a month, my drinks went from two or three in a night to four or five, and ultimately, to enough to black out.

After hours of reading and reflecting on the ups and downs of my drinking experience, there'd been no question in my mind about going to the meeting with Jason the next morning on Sunday, December 3.

The experience at that meeting was far different than the feeling I'd had while devouring the pages of the book, which is universally known in recovery as The Big Book. Luckily for me, when the woman leading my first meeting in Charlotte asked if anyone had a topic, Jason spoke.

"This is my buddy's first meeting," he said to the room. "So, what would you tell a newcomer in their first meeting?"

From that point, the meeting seemed divinely designed for me to realize I wasn't like these alcoholics. The stories I was hearing weren't even in the same universe as my extremely flawed, but relatively tame-by-comparison failures.

Multiple DUIs. Years in prison. Broken families. Dire illness.

I had fallen down once walking home along North Avenue from Atkins Park, a bar on Highland Avenue, and fibbed about my busted-open knee and the gash across my nose. "Damn Atlanta sidewalks," I'd lied. I'd driven drunk maybe half a dozen times, sent embarrassing and inappropriate texts, thrown up in an Uber, broken a finger falling in the hallway leading to my apartment, and most shamefully, I'd made unwanted advances toward female friends during parties and fundraisers.

I was, *of course*, deeply ashamed of these inexcusable failures where the common thread was excessive alcohol consumption, and I was *deeply* grateful that I'd been able to push through darkly vivid and dangerously convincing suicidal ideas and plans to ultimately find my way to AA.

But, here in my first meeting, it seemed that my struggles were worlds away from what these strangers were describing. This meeting seemed divinely intended to trick me into believing that I was "better" than they were, because somehow the wreckage of my alcoholism hadn't landed *me* in jail, in the hospital, or worse.

Luckily, my barely sober brain called bullshit. I snapped back to reality. Yes, I hadn't experienced the kinds of consequences I was hearing shared around this room. *Yet.*

In the middle of the meeting, I decided I was done building my alcoholic resume. I hated the mistakes I'd made. I hated myself for hurting people I cared about. And while my mistakes couldn't be undone, I could control one thing: no future failure would be because I was drunk.

In that moment, I decided I was done with alcohol. No more bourbon. No more shots. No more wine pairings. No more blackouts. No more drunk driving. No more embarrassing texts. No more disrespecting my friends. No more destroyed friendships. No more wreckage.

Shortly before the meeting ended, a round, white, plastic poker chip with AA in gold lettering emblazoned across the middle was offered to anyone "wanting to try this way of life."

I didn't hesitate.

It's my only white chip. It's one of my prized possessions. It has saved my life, and I hope I'm never in the situation where I need to pick up another one because I've relapsed.

During the preceding few years leading up to that meeting, the person I hoped to be and the person I actually was on a daily basis had inched farther and farther away from each other, until I'd ended up in a place where I didn't recognize the lost soul staring back at me in the mirror.

But I didn't deserve to be sentenced to death at my own hands.

In taking that chip, I not only began an attempt to transform into the person I hoped to be, but I unknowingly did what my dad was unable to do.

I asked for help.

The first step of Alcoholics Anonymous reads: "We admitted we were powerless over alcohol—that our lives had become unmanageable."

On February 23, 1996, when he was writing the letters he left us and planning his final act, my dad's life had become unmanageable.

On November 29, 2017, it became clear to me that my life had become unmanageable, too.

Steve Romig ended his life. Instead, after brushing up against my own suicide, I pushed through the pain and shame and failure and I asked for help, in order to work to live a better version of my life through sobriety.

Did I veer off his path with my choice? Was I ever on it in the first place? There's no way to know either answer, but I believe that in accepting that white chip—and establishing myself in AA-based sobriety—I did what he couldn't do.

I chose life.

I was amazingly lost. I was filled with shame. I was terrified. I was more flawed than I'd ever imagined.

But I didn't want to die.

I wanted to live a better life.

I wanted to be a better person.

I wanted to stop drinking and start healing.

With that white chip, I began to do just that.

And with this AA meeting in Atlanta on runoff Election Day, I found my first home group, which was essential in giving my early sobriety the foundation needed to ultimately transform my life.

February 8, 2020

Treasure the farmer.
—Alice Waters, *The Art of Simple Food II*

M Y TWO YEARS of working in Georgia's good food movement
have rooted my heart and mind in this value statement.

When most people think of farming, they think of the endless, vast, mono-crop fields that Audrey and I used to drive past in the middle-of-nowhere Indiana on the way back to South Carolina from South Bend. But for generations, small-scale farmers all over the country have operated sustainable fruit and vegetable operations. Today, these operations can be found on rural, urban, and suburban acreage, and the farmers offer their produce at farmers markets, through weekly CSA box subscriptions, and to local restaurants committed to purchasing from local farms.

At Georgia Organics, the farmers we work to support are also artists and community organizers and small business owners. They're a cross-section of the best of humanity as they work tirelessly to feed their communities while doing more than their part as committed stewards of the earth.

Alice Waters didn't invent the idea of buying locally from small farmers. But in 1971, after Americans had spent the previous two decades embracing canned vegetables, powdered potatoes, and aluminum trays filled with "TV dinners," she opened Chez Panisse in Berkeley, California, bringing the concept of seasonal, farm-fresh menus into the world of fine dining.

Later, almost 25 years after opening Chez Panisse, Waters founded the Edible Schoolyard Project at the Martin Luther King, Jr. Middle School in Berkeley. Her mission was to connect children to fresh, healthy food by teaching them to grow, harvest, and prepare food from their own school garden.

On this surprisingly snowy Saturday in Athens, Georgia, Alice Waters was sitting at the other end of the table from me. This was thanks to the tireless coordination of our dynamic events manager, Ashley, fundraising by our transformative CEO, also named Alice, and a longstanding friendship with one of our board members, Matthew, who personally invited Chef Waters to travel across the country to share her vision with the attendees at the annual Georgia Organics Conference & Expo. Today, she was leading our guests through a simulated school lunch, so they could personally experience the ideal cafeteria-based learning-while-eating experience for kids.

Instead of the lunches of pizza-and-fries I'd eaten at E. L. Wright Middle School, we shared Georgia peanut hummus with flatbread, a local green salad with Meyer lemon vinaigrette, sautéed collards, root vegetables, cornbread, and the most luscious apple crisp and vanilla ice cream you can imagine.

Not only did the 650 people in attendance hear Waters share her transformative perspective on local, healthy food, but she had now joined me and my communications team for a podcast interview, so that we could share her voice and her message more broadly across Georgia and the internet through the Atlanta Foodcast.

"I wanted to present a school lunch that is the kind that I envision for the public school system," the 76-year-old good-food pioneer told podcast host, Ben. "I wanted to dispel the myths that there's no time for kids to sit at a table to eat lunch, and that it's impossible to serve wholesome food."

The farm-to-school work that Waters began leading nationally in the mid-1990s sprouted up in Georgia in 2007 through the work and vision of Georgia Organics. In fact, my first engagement with our organization had been working with its kind but badass advocacy director, Jennifer, on farm-to-school legislation during the 2011 legislative session; I'd been a legislative aide for Decatur's Democratic State Rep. Stephanie Stuckey, a strong legislative ally for policies that enabled farm-to-school education to grow in Georgia's public schools. By the 2018–19 school year, before the pandemic, more than 50 percent of Georgia's school districts were participating in farm-to-school education, teaching children to embrace healthy, local food in their cafeterias and classrooms through learning, growing, and eating.

As a kid, my limited understanding of farming and fresh, local vegetables had come from my grandfather.

In 1981, Bee and Papa had built a modest, two-bedroom, two-bath, one-story house on a 400-acre plot of land near Blythewood, South Carolina, that the Riley family had lived on since the 1890s—a century before we grew up there waiting for Santa Claus, searching for Easter eggs, and skipping rocks across the ankle-high water of the creek we loved exploring.

My great-grandfather, Joseph Riley, had run a modest dairy farm and small vegetable operation there during the early 1900s, where his seven children learned to plant and harvest and tend to the cows. "Sundays were always occupied with churchgoing, along with milking, both morning and evening," Papa wrote in the notes for his unfinished memoir. "My father was often heard to say, 'We'll work the garden out on Sunday afternoon—while we rest.'"

When we were kids, Papa had kept a chicken coop full of hens that would give us fresh, light-green eggs—and lots of background noise when I was on the phone in middle school, which my friend

Shannon always lovingly teased me about. Papa had also maintained a large garden, where we helped him gather green beans, tomatoes and, for some reason, yellow squash (which he loved, and I still despise).

"Papa likes to plant the seeds and watch them grow," Bee wrote of his gardening commitment. "The best thing about the finished product is sharing the foods with our family and friends. He probably gives away more than he keeps!"

My love of, and connection to, Southern food developed in Bee and Papa's kitchen through scarfing down country-cooking delicacies like salty country ham, eaten straight from a still-sizzling cast iron skillet; hot cornbread, fresh from the oven and covered in butter and honey; pots of stewed pole beans and tomatoes and okra; and Bee's desserts—specifically, my favorite cake, which alternated fluffy layers of white cake and perfectly sweet, light brown chocolate buttercream icing.

I'm extremely fortunate to have inherited both Bee's talent for writing and Papa's proficiency in and around a stove. While cooking is now a passion and an escape for me, it actually wasn't something I did too much of before I moved into my own apartment during my sophomore year of college in Tuscaloosa. In the years since that first kitchen (in which I had to rely on an electric skillet for making everything from pancakes to chili to Mom's shrimp creole), I've not only become more proficient as a home cook, but I've also become more invested in seasonal eating and buying from local farmers.

The only thing that calms my anxiety and sidelines my depression more than methodically organizing, prepping, and cooking a homemade meal is the time spent first, on a beautiful Saturday or Sunday morning, picking out the ingredients for that meal at one of the small farmers markets in Atlanta. I escape by designing and preparing ambitious meals, but even more by connecting with the farmers that brought those ingredients into the world to feed our community.

This wasn't my life before I started working for Georgia Organics in January 2018, only weeks after I'd stopped drinking. Sure, I'd cooked with fresh ingredients from Publix or Whole Foods, and it had calmed my nerves. But I've discovered that there's a massive difference for me when I cook with produce that I purchased from a farmer I know, sustainably grown meat from an essential farm like White Oak Pastures in Bluffton, Georgia, or locally harvested grains like Carolina Gold Rice from Anson Mills in Columbia.

But far more than just my cooking changed when I joined the 21-year-old nonprofit. Running a close second to the sobriety I was maintaining through AA, Georgia Organics saved my life.

The opportunity given to me to lead fundraising at Georgia Organics came less than three weeks after my first AA meeting, and less than two months before I was diagnosed with tongue cancer. It turned out to be the perfect place to give me the stability needed to become healthy in mind, body, and spirit as I began a sober life and moved from cancer diagnosis through surgery to remission.

Now, as Chef Waters encourages us to do with the first words from *The Art of Simple Food II*, I truly treasure farmers because of the work they do to take care of our environment, our communities, our cultures, our minds, and our bodies. Through that newfound perspective and personal investment, I've found infinitely more enjoyment and connection and flavor in my cooking, bringing new elements of happiness and peace into my frenetic life each week.

But more than anything, I treasure Georgia Organics, all my coworkers, and my new friends in Georgia's good food movement. As a whole, they've given me the stability and support that I need in order to continue to work toward being the best version of myself, so I can be treasured too.

October 5, 2012

BOTTLES, BEER, AND even batteries hurtled over our heads onto Turner Field for almost 19 minutes.

Audrey and I had been sitting 12 rows from third base for this one-game playoff between the Braves and the St. Louis Cardinals; it was going to be the last game of legendary third baseman Chipper Jones if our Braves didn't find a way to win. Now we were standing with our backs to the field to take in the fury and chaos of a full house of livid Braves fans, while keeping alert for any projectiles coming in our direction. They just kept coming.

This was the first year of Major League Baseball's expanded playoffs. Before 2012, the winner of the Wild Card had automatically played in the best-of-five National League Division Series. Instead, this was the first all-or-nothing Wild Card game in baseball history. Minutes earlier, before play was halted by the barrage of trash flying onto the field, the game was in the bottom of the eighth inning and the Braves were down 6–3 with one out. Atlanta catcher David Ross was at first and second baseman Dan Uggla was on second.

Our 22-year-old, slick-fielding shortstop Andrelton Simmons had just hit an arcing pop-up into left field that would fall between the Cardinals shortstop, Pete Kozma, and left fielder Matt Holliday, about 50 feet past the infield dirt.

Left-field umpire Sam Holbrook had watched Kozma attempt to track Simmons's pop fly, and for some reason—only known to the sports gods who loathe Atlanta—had called Simmons out on the infield fly rule.

Major League Baseball Rule 2.00 defines an infield fly as a fair fly ball (not including a line drive or an attempted bunt) that can be caught by an infielder *with ordinary effort*, when first and second, or first, second, and third bases are occupied, before two are out. (The point of the rule is to keep infielders from choosing to let the ball drop, thereby turning it into a double play.)

Note that wording: "with ordinary effort."

"I'm a shortstop," Simmons later told the press. "I've had the infield fly rule happen many times. But never in left. Maybe in the shallow part of the outfield. But never in the middle of left field."

To even attempt the play, Simmons would have had to make more than "ordinary" effort. But on this play, a terrible call not only killed a potential Braves rally—it triggered 19 minutes of chaos like I'd never experienced during a sporting event. It was truly bananas. All we could do was watch, and dodge the projectiles flying from the stadium's upper deck.

I love the intricacies of baseball and its on-field and off-field stories. I love the pace and grace of the game. I love that it's one of the few things that has the ability to soften my anxiety. I love the numbers and statistics and strategy. I love the way it felt to turn a double play from second base, or hit a ball over the fence, and the jubilant connection with my teammates that immediately followed those on-field successes. I love that watching a game can immediately connect me to those moments, bringing a smile to my face and joy to my heart. I love the Cubs, and I love the Braves.

But most of all, I love that it was a cornerstone of my relationship with Bee, who had died less than two months before this game, from complications due to Alzheimer's.

Bee listened to every Braves game on the radio for decades, even after cable became a thing (because they couldn't get it at their home), and she instilled in me a deep love for the Braves during the mid-1980s, when the team was pretty terrible. But she wasn't ever deterred by their futility.

She pulled for Dale Murphy and "her Braves" every day through the abysmal teams of the late 1980s (which, from 1985 through 1989, won only 324 games while losing 480—a paltry winning percentage of 40.3). The 1989 Braves finished out the decade with only 63 wins (nine more than in their wretched 1988 season, when they'd gone 54–106), earning them the first overall pick in the 1990 amateur draft. While the Braves were terrible, I'd focused on the Cubs. Until 1990.

On June 4, 1990, the Braves were continuing to struggle on the field, losing 6–0 to Los Angeles at Dodger Stadium, as Ramon Martinez struck out 18 Braves while allowing only three hits. Off the field, however, it was a day that changed the franchise, and anything but another summer day for me.

We'd just finished a family trip to Disney World in Orlando—where, thankfully, I hadn't thrown up while riding on Space Mountain—and were stopping on our way back to Columbia to visit one of Mom's childhood friends, who lived in DeLand, Florida.

Up to and including this point in my 12 years, I'd loved baseball above all else. I'd watched the Cubs on WGN in the afternoon, the Braves on TBS in the evening, *Baseball Tonight* every night, and as many other games on ESPN as I could consume. I'd played baseball. I'd collected baseball cards. I'd religiously read *Baseball America*. Baseball gave me life. It was my first love.

So that day, I'd thought it was so cool that, on the day the Braves drafted high school shortstop Larry "Chipper" Jones with their Number One overall draft pick, I was in his hometown.

From then on, I'd followed Chipper through the minors, up until his brief big-league debut in the final stretch of the 1993 season. He'd

become one of my favorite players, and the first one I would follow for his entire career: from the moment he stepped on the field
in a Braves uniform on September 11, 1993, as Jeff Blauser's defensive replacement at shortstop in a blowout win over the San Diego
Padres, until the moment he walked off to a standing ovation at the
end of this game.

I'd specifically purchased these seats in line with third base, so
Audrey and I could watch the final innings of the first player I'd truly
followed from draft day to retirement.

When Chipper walked off the field after the Braves' Wild Card
loss, 19 years had passed since his first game in 1993. In 1995, his
first full season after missing strike-shortened 1994 with a torn ACL,
the rookie third baseman had helped lead Atlanta to its only World
Series championship.

In what would be the last baseball game my dad ever saw, the
Braves had defeated the Cleveland Indians 1–0 in Game Six on
October 28, 1995, behind eight shutout innings from fellow future
Hall of Fame starting pitcher Tom Glavine and a solo home run from
right fielder David Justice.

Chipper achieved so much on the baseball field, but nothing
sums up his career better than the inscription on his plaque hanging
between contemporaries Vladimir Guerrero and Jim Thome in the
Baseball Hall of Fame in Cooperstown, NY, where he was inducted
on July 29, 2018.

Larry Wayne Jones Jr.

"Chipper"

Atlanta, N. L. 1993, 1995–2012

> "Switch-hitting lineup centerpiece during the Braves' dynas-
> tic seasons of the 1990s and 2000s. Among players who were
> primarily third basemen, retired as the all-time leader in runs
> scored and driven in. Batted better than .300 from both sides
> of the plate during 19-year career. Totaling 468 home runs,

1,623 RBI and eight All-Star Game selections. First overall pick in 1990 Draft, fueled Braves to 1995 championship as dynamic rookie. Hit 45 home runs in 1999 N. L. MVP season and won 2008 batting crown with .364 average. Only switch-hitter in history with at least .300 batting average, .400 on-base percentage and .500 slugging percentage."

But, in a baseball-geek story that I love for its actual ending and impact, Chipper almost hadn't been the Braves' pick.

Leading up to our Disney trip in June 1990, the rumor had been circulating that Atlanta, which was building a pitching-first club, coveted hard-throwing right-handed Texas high schooler Todd Van Poppel, who'd allegedly said that if picked by Atlanta, he'd stay home and pitch at the University of Texas. "I really have no doubt that if Todd Van Poppel would have shown any interest at all, he probably would have been taken by the Braves," Chipper's dad, Larry Jones Sr., said in *Tales from the Atlanta Braves Dugout* by Cory McCartney.

But no interest was shown. And on June 3, the day before the draft, Braves general manager Bobby Cox—who would begin his second stint as Braves manager on June 22, 1990, and in 1991 would lead the team to the first of 14 straight N. L. East Titles—had called the Van Poppels to let them know the Braves would be passing on Todd in the next day's draft.

Van Poppel was ultimately selected, 13 picks after Chipper, by the Oakland Athletics, didn't become a Longhorn, and made his fast-tracked debut in the majors as a 19-year-old on September 11, 1991—two years to the day before Chipper pinch-ran for Blauser. He struck out five and gave up five runs that day. As compared to Chipper's Hall of Fame career, after five seasons in Oakland, Van Poppel bounced around the majors for six seasons before retiring in 2004 with a record of 40–52, a 5.58 ERA, a 1.55 WHIP, and 711 strikeouts in 907 innings pitched.

The Braves had finished last again in 1990—winning 65 games—but ultimately had won the year by drafting Chipper and securing his Hall of Fame impact for the next two decades in both the middle of the Braves lineup and their clubhouse.

After this loss to the Cardinals in what is still known as "The Infield Fly Game," Chipper wasn't willing to blame the blown call for the Braves' loss. "Ultimately, I think that when we look back on this loss, we need to look at ourselves in the mirror," said Jones as quoted by Jayson Stark in his game story for ESPN. "We put ourselves in that predicament. [So] I'm not willing to say that that particular call cost us the ballgame."

As a City of Atlanta resident and lifelong Braves fan, there was nowhere I would have rather been that Friday night. Despite the craziness of the experience, it was an honor to participate in Chipper's final standing ovation as his exemplary career came to a close.

If only I could have gone home and called Bee to give her all the details.

August 23, 1998

THE CLERK AT Capitol Newsstand on O'Neil Court wasn't sure what to make of my buying a stack of 20 Sunday papers.

The State wasn't just my new employer. It was the largest daily newspaper in South Carolina. It had been a staple of my childhood, where I read Braves and Cubs box scores before school as I devoured my yellow Tupperware bowl full of Cinnamon Toast Crunch. If ink was in my blood, it had arrived there through a childhood poring over *The State*'s sports section.

I spent 20 dollars on newspapers that morning because of the significance of five words.

By Jeff Romig

Special Correspondent

Less than six weeks earlier, I'd still been living in Tuscaloosa, waiting tables at Northport Diner, and preparing to transfer back home to Columbia to finish college at USC.

Part of my decision to move home had been the desire to work in some capacity on a daily newspaper while I earned my bachelor's degree in Journalism. I'd figured this was more likely in Columbia than Tuscaloosa because *The State* had a larger circulation than *The Tuscaloosa News*. So, I'd assumed there might be more opportunities for kid reporters like me.

Luckily, I was right.

A few days after I'd settled into my one-bedroom apartment off Greystone Boulevard near Riverbanks Zoo, I'd dressed up as nicely as I could—khakis and an American Eagle button-up shirt—and driven to *The State*'s headquarters on Shop Road, a stone's throw away from Williams-Brice Stadium, where I'd watched mostly mediocre Gamecocks football since the 1980s.

My goal was to share in person my resume and portfolio of clips, representing everything from my college writing for *The Crimson White* to my first high school work from *The Viking Shield*.

I'd walked into the Human Resources office, asked if I could talk to someone in charge of hiring, and declared my desire to work there. I'm not sure if what I'd been was confident or just ridiculous, but whatever I'd been, minutes later I'd found myself talking to Beverly, a gracious editor who for some reason had agreed to talk to this 20-year-old kid who'd walked in off the street.

I'd handed her my portfolio and answered her questions, telling her I'd love to work in sports, but was open to any opportunity that was available. Beverly had thanked me for coming and said she'd be in touch. I hadn't had extremely high hopes; I'd figured I'd soon be waiting tables at Villa Tronco again, as I had before I moved to Alabama in 1996.

When I returned to my apartment less than an hour later, I'd discovered a message on my answering machine from the sports editor at *The State,* asking to call him back. I'd done so without hesitation, and he'd invited me to interview.

It shouldn't have been this easy, but the stars seemed aligned, and early the next week, I'd driven back to *The State.*

Invited this time, I'd walked up the stairs to the second-floor newsroom and had been escorted back to the sports department, where I was formally introduced to Brian, the sports editor with whom I'd briefly spoken on the phone. He'd told me he had an open position for an agate clerk, a job designed to digitally create the sports section's scoreboard portion, where standings, transactions, and box scores appeared.

It didn't pay that much and was only two nights each week from 6 to 11 p.m., but I would have done it for free.

Brian had said the job was mine if I wanted it, but he wanted to be clear—this wasn't a writing position: I would design the scoreboard, take phone calls, and do whatever the editors needed. I didn't care what the caveats were. I hadn't hesitated in accepting when he offered me the job that officially made a professional newsroom my workplace.

The night I started, I was introduced to Brent, the other agate clerk, who worked a five-night-a-week version of my new job and was instructed to train me. Brent was also a USC journalism student and, to my surprise, as we began training, he'd asked me if I wanted to have his five-night role. He'd wanted to cut back on nights to cover minor league baseball and focus on graduating. I'd jumped at the opportunity, and before I knew it Brian had agreed to swap our roles. In a blink, I had a 25-hour-a-week job instead of a 10-hour one.

I'd learned the basics of design in high school, so I took to my new role quickly, working clean and fast, and impressing my editors with my never-say-no approach. As a result, when Brent couldn't cover the Capital City Bombers on Saturday, August 22 as they took on the Macon Braves, I'd been given my first writing assignment— to cover a Braves game!

My first experience covering a game as a professional was exciting at the park and then at the paper. The Bombers had rallied in the ninth to tie the game 5–5, before ultimately losing 7–5 to future Braves second baseman Marcus Giles's team in 14 innings. The extra-long game ate up most of my writing time, so I only had about 20 minutes to write my game story once I returned to the newsroom. But I'd focused, and finished my story just before the 12:15 a.m. deadline.

Now, with 20 copies of *The State* confirming my byline's existence and 20 fewer dollars in my wallet, I drove to join my family at Beulah United Methodist Church, near Bee and Papa's house, to celebrate their 50th wedding anniversary. It was a modest luncheon for friends and family, offering two of our grandparents' favorite entrées from the Ramada: sticky, sweet baby back ribs and a lasagna in a massive tray.

Bee and Papa had met in Myrtle Beach in 1947, when he joined his friend, Billy, to pick up Bee's friend Hilda. Their life together began with this blind date, and they were married on August 28, 1948. In *Grandmother Remembers*, a book Bee gave me in 1985 to chronicle our family, she wrote that she liked Papa because "he was kind, interesting, and handsome." In Papa's notes for his memoir, he wrote of her: "It was her love that unlocked every door in my heart."

I was so excited to share my first story with them as an impromptu 50th anniversary surprise, and from that day on, Bee would save my sports stories, always lovingly circling my byline on the articles she cut out of her copy of *The State*.

June 1, 1996

WHEN DAD HAD been a partner at the law firm of McDonald, McKenzie, Rubin, Miller & Lybrand, his office view was one of the best in Columbia.

The firm sits directly across Main Street from the Richland County Judicial Center. Dad's office was on the Blanding Street side and shared an alley with our family's favorite restaurant, Villa Tronco. Technically, all you saw from his window was a wall. But the promise of the magical cuisine being served on the wall's other side made it a beautiful view, indeed.

Square, crispy thin-crust pizza with sausage, pepperoni, ground beef, onions, green peppers, and mushrooms, all bound together by gooey, melted mozzarella over sweet-and-tart tomato sauce.

Sizzling veal saltimbocca, layered with prosciutto, sage, mozzarella, and mushrooms and simmered in white wine.

Perfectly supple Oreo cheesecake, packed with creaminess and a bit of crumble in every rich bite.

I visited the alley before everyone began arriving for lunch, to touch his window and remember him for a moment. As I stood there, I wished that he could still see that view. He had left the firm in 1995, the year before he died, but those would always be his window and his office to me.

Dad was supposed to be with us at Villa Tronco for this Saturday's lunch to celebrate my graduation from Spring Valley High School the day before. I'd made it through high school, and in less than three months, I'd be running away to Tuscaloosa to start college at The University of Alabama. But he was gone, and I wondered what could have been.

What would he have said to me after graduation? What would he have said about me to the roomful of our friends and family at today's lunch? Would he have been proud?

There was no way to know, but I couldn't stop thinking about the possibilities as family and friends gathered to celebrate me, just 97 days after his suicide.

His unmistakable absence had to be on everyone's mind, but pizza, pasta, and cheesecake were enticing, even if only momentary, distractions.

That lunch was the latest of many important meals of my life spent at Villa Tronco. Columbia's first and longest-operating Italian restaurant, it had been opened in 1940 on Blanding Street in an abandoned 19th Century firehouse. It's a special place to our family, and a Columbia institution.

In the 10 years before opening Villa Tronco, James and "Mama" Sadie Tronco had introduced pizza and Italian food to Columbia from their fruit store on Main Street by feeding Italian-American soldiers stationed at Fort Jackson, who were homesick and hungry for red-sauce favorites like spaghetti and meatballs. The Troncos' Iodine Fruit Store had eventually become Tony's Spaghetti House, and then Villa Tronco when they opened in the firehouse on Blanding. Until her 1988 death at 87, Mama Tronco had stayed involved with the trattoria, while her daughter Carmella and husband Henry, a USC basketball legend, delivered authentic Italian food to Columbia.

Mama Tronco's granddaughter (also named Carmella) and her husband, Joe, now operated the restaurant. They were our family friends; Joe had grown up with my Uncle Wally and had been a frequent tennis partner for him and Dad. The week after the luncheon, I'd be joining their staff as a server during lunch service.

Villa Tronco had always felt like home, and my first-ever job would show me the inner workings of a restaurant and give me lifelong respect for restaurant workers. It would also teach me how to sneak and eat makeshift sandwiches of salami stuffed inside a hot, soft, cannoli-shaped roll. Those rolls were provided at the beginning of the meal to every table, alongside a just-dressed-enough vinaigrette salad of crisp lettuce, juicy cherry tomato halves, and hand-diced provolone cheese.

As the oldest grandson, I was the first of the four cousins in our family to graduate from high school. The adults called us "the cousins," but technically, we were two sets of siblings, each of us two years apart—the birth order alternating between the two families of the Riley sisters, Sandra Romig (my mom) and Pam Cates (my aunt). My cousin Gina was two years behind me, my brother Bryan two years behind her, and Gina's sister Abby two years behind Bryan.

The Cates girls and Romig boys had basically been raised as siblings, spending Easter, Thanksgiving, and Christmas—along with countless Sunday lunches after church—together in "the country," as we called Bee and Papa's rural Richland County home.

On this day, we were all together for the first of our four eventual high school graduation lunches at Villa Tronco. With one glaring exception, our entire extended Columbia family was there, along with our Charleston family, who'd driven up for the day. At least one of Dad's law partners joined, along with close family friends from church and my girlfriend. Dad's parents, Ruth and Clarence, even came from Illinois to be there for the festivities. But each guest only reminded me of the person who was supposed to be there, but had decided on February 24 that he wouldn't attend.

I was still so angry; I wouldn't find my way through that fury for a very long time.

The K–12 chapter of my life was now officially closed: I was a high school graduate. Next week, I would start my first paid job in the very space we were having lunch. And in 10 weeks, I'd leave all of these wonderful people, gathered to support me at Villa Tronco, when I moved six hours west to Tuscaloosa.

It seemed like everything was possible, but, at the same time, so much was now impossible.

As my relationship with my dad became more and more strained during my teen years, I'd always looked forward to the day after graduation. This milestone was supposed to be the beginning of a new era; I would be an adult, and maybe he and I would be friends again.

I always thought that would be our future.

It didn't matter that he worked all the time.

It didn't matter that when we talked, we fought.

It didn't matter because it was sure to change. Right?

The future that was supposed to start today was now impossible because of his final choice, and his rationale for it.

"I am sorry that I have to write this letter and you have to read it," Dad had begun his suicide letter to me. "But I made a decision that I felt was best for all of you and me as well."

Unknown to me then, my future would always include the version of him seared in my mind through his words and final act. I wouldn't truly understand the power that they had to destroy me again and again for years. And it would take even longer to drain them of that power.

June 22, 2012

WRITING WALLY'S OBITUARY would be the most difficult writing assignment of my life so far. My words would simultaneously attempt to honor him, while crushing me.

Audrey and I woke up on the morning of our 10th wedding anniversary to learn the heartbreaking news that Wally was gone after his second battle with pancreatic cancer. He fought bravely and without complaint, but his fight had ended around 3 a.m. Pam selected me to write his obituary to share him with the world a final time.

Wally Cates wasn't just any uncle, as Pam isn't just any aunt. The Cates and Romig families grew up together as part of the Riley clan, with my grandparents Papa and Bee playing active roles in the lives of their daughters Pam and Sandra, their sons-in-law Wally and Steve, and their four grandchildren: Bryan, Gina, Abby, and me.

This was our family. The two couples were best friends, and the four kids were essentially siblings. We grew up attending North Trenholm Baptist Church together. We spent holidays together, often ate Sunday lunch together, and vacationed together. And when my dad ended his life, Wally and Pam had scooped up our family and taken care of us.

Wally had been like a second dad to me and especially to Bryan, who was only 13 when Dad died. I wasn't good at asking for help or showing appreciation for the help I was given. But I was grateful that Wally moved me to college in Tuscaloosa in August 1996 and then back to Columbia in July 1998, when I transferred to USC. I was even more grateful that he didn't make me pay for the damage I did to his prized white Mercedes in 1990. I had accidently slammed into it while I was badly driving Bee and Papa's golf cart, which they mainly used to drive from their house to get the mail and ride around the grassy hills on their homestead.

Wally loved Pam. He loved his girls, his son-in-law Josh, and his grandchildren Jackson, Riley Cates, and Rutherford, the grandson he would never meet. He also loved his extended family, his church and tennis families, and his Gamecocks.

A few days later, during Wally's memorial service, our family friend Luke, who was giving the eulogy, called Wally his best friend. Across the church there were more men who could say the same. That was Wally—a great man and great friend. My dad didn't have lots of close friends. But Wally was his best friend, and Dad would have been so proud of Wally for how hard he fought, and he would have been so grateful to Wally for taking care of his family for the past 16 years.

As Wally lay in a coma the night before he died, I had a final chance to thank him for everything he'd done for us, and to tell him how much we loved him and would miss him. Before I said good-bye, I told him that I was sure Steve had a tennis court ready for them in heaven.

When we buried Wally, we were able to place fresh flowers on my dad's grave, because these two old friends were buried in line with each other in our family plot. But they're also not there; they're in a better place, playing all the tennis they want without any pain in their minds or bodies.

March 4, 2000

I COULDN'T BELIEVE WHAT I'd just witnessed.

For the rest of my life, it might stand as the most incredible single-game performance I'd ever see in person. And it was *definitely* going to be my lead for today's story from Sumter, where I'd been assigned to spend Saturday watching six high school basketball championship games that matched up teams from South Carolina Independent School Association (SCISA) private schools from across the state.

I was only to write one story, and it was expected to be from one of the three boys' games.

A senior guard named Nancy changed that.

Nancy, who'd committed to play basketball on scholarship at Auburn University, scored every single point for her team in its 40–30 championship victory over Avalon Academy, while also pulling down 17 rebounds. With straight faces, she and her coach agreed it wasn't her greatest game.

"I always dreamed I'd go out with my best game," said Nancy, who'd scored 4,238 points in her high school career. "That didn't happen, but with a state championship, that was sweet enough."

My editor, Fred, seemed surprised, but supported my decision to lead with Nancy's jaw-dropping performance.

I'd begun writing high school sports stories for Fred within months of joining *The State* in August 1998. Working five nights a week on the sports desk, I'd become his go-to features writer for Richland School District Two, where I'd spent my K–12 years and still had many relationships.

I pitched stories about friends I'd played baseball with and against, friends with whom I went to church, and other teens with great stories I learned about from former teachers, coaches, and friends with district connections.

One of my first feature stories—and still one of my favorites— was about my friend Kasey. She was a star tennis, basketball, *and* softball player for Richland Northeast, the rival of my high school, Spring Valley. Our families were friends from church; and from 1990 through 1992, we'd observed little Kasey's resilience as she went through treatment for leukemia while in elementary school.

She was the first person in my personal life who had battled cancer and won. While she was in treatment, she'd made friends with Duke basketball coach Mike Krzyzewski. They had met in 1992 at a matchup in which Duke played and beat Clemson. Coach K, having been notified about Kasey's cancer and presence, sat and talked with Kasey after Duke's victory for 10 minutes before his players, including star center Christian Laettner, joined them to introduce themselves to her.

"That was the best thing that came out of having leukemia," Kasey had told me in 1998 for the profile I wrote on her for *The State*. "The night I went to Clemson was probably the best night of my life."

Kasey did incredible things between the lines, but she was always an inspiration to me and the world for her resolve and poise outside her three fields of play.

My ability to proactively pitch my own feature stories had led to me working 40-hour weeks at *The State* while I went to USC. I wrote features in my free time, even writing a preview of my high school baseball team at Spring Valley, referencing guys I'd played with just a few years before. On nights off, Fred would send me to cover basketball, where I watched one of the most exciting players I'd ever seen.

During the 1999–2000 high school basketball season, the Columbia High School girls team received as much coverage as most of the boys' teams in town because of star, Rutgers-bound point guard Nikki, who sliced through opposing defenses with ease, and could seemingly score at will from anywhere on the court as she led the Capitals to a state championship that Spring.

Covering high school sports taught me that compelling stories exist everywhere, and almost always where they're not expected. It was through writing these features and game stories, and dozens like them, that I truly began to hone my craft as a storyteller.

April 9, 2002

HANK AARON DIDN'T want to talk about Barry Bonds.

It was the day after the 28th anniversary of Hank hitting home run number 715 in Fulton County Stadium to eclipse Babe Ruth's career total of 714, and everyone wanted to know what Hank thought of Bonds's chances to break his record of 755 career home runs. By hitting 73 home runs in 2001, Bonds had broken Mark McGwire's single-season record, and he'd now already hit five more in the first four games of the 2002 season, giving him 572 lifetime homers at age 37. (Bonds ultimately broke Hank's record in 2007, finishing his career with 762 home runs.)

But Hammerin' Hank wasn't in Greenville to talk baseball.

Today was about BMW.

BMW had established its American manufacturing plant in Spartanburg County to great fanfare in 1992. Seven years later, after being recruited by BMW, Hank had opened his BMW dealership in Union City, a predominantly Black Atlanta suburb. In its first 12 months of operation, Hank Aaron BMW had proven that the brand could thrive in diverse locations, exceeding corporate sales projections by 27 percent. Hank had also made it his priority to hire a Black general manager.

"I was bent on doing that," Aaron told me, after speaking on a minority small business development panel at the Southern Automotive Manufacturing Conference. "We like to make sure we give Black leaders a chance to move up. (They) are capable of doing anything. It has a positive influence on the aspirations and the self-expectations of the people who live in that community."

Covering BMW Manufacturing Corporation as part of my business-writing beat at the *Herald-Journal* was one of my prized experiences during my newspaper career, and not simply because it allowed me to interview the greatest Atlanta Braves player in history and one of baseball's all-time greats. Rather, it was because I was able to tell interesting and unexpected stories about BMW.

But the absolute best thing about covering BMW was being able to work with Bunny Richardson, who led corporate communications at the Spartanburg plant for 17 years, from 1995 to 2012. Bunny, who was 63 when she died of cancer in 2014, was a fellow USC Journalism School grad and former Assistant Managing Editor at *The State*, where I'd started my newspaper career. Bunny was my main contact and source at BMW, and was wonderful to work with because she loved and respected journalists so much.

I wrote dozens of BMW stories during my 30 months with the *Herald-Journal*, but my favorite would be the front-page exclusive I would write on April 13, 2002.

Three days after my story about Hank Aaron had been published, I was working to break the story of the new BMW roadster's name. I called Bunny to confirm the details only after I had the name, specs, and price of the plant's new model confirmed by multiple sources. Her response was that she would "neither confirm nor deny" my reporting. Her "nor deny" wording was revealing because Bunny would never lie to a reporter about anything.

After my story ran under the headline "BMW's Z4 a Secret No More," I found a message when I arrived at my desk at the *Herald-Journal* on Monday morning, asking me to call Bunny.

At first, panic set in, because my anxiety wanted to deceive me into believing that I'd messed something up. But when Bunny answered, she graciously shared with me how impressed she was with my sourcing and reporting. From an old newspaper pro like Bunny, it was the highest compliment I could have received.

I told her exactly that, six months later when we were eating lunch at a small café in the North Carolina mountains. National auto media had been invited to the BMW plant to drive the new Z4 from Greenville to the mountain town of Hendersonville on back roads. It was a clear, cool autumn day as I wound through the mountainous curves with the top down, driving this magnificent machine while orange, yellow, and red leaves flew over my head. As I drove back to Greenville, I grabbed my cell phone and dialed up my best friend, Jason, who was at law school in freezing Ann Arbor, Michigan, to brag that I was behind the wheel of a new BMW convertible, soaking up the beautiful weather.

It was a perfect day: covering my favorite company, eating lunch with one of my favorite people, driving a BMW for the first time, and reflecting on that week six months earlier, which had begun with my interviewing Hank Aaron and ended with me impressing Bunny Richardson. I can't think of a better example of the passions, people, and experiences that keep me alive all coming together so magically into one story.

August 4, 2012

E VEN THOUGH YOU would think a grief camp for kids would produce more tears than smiles, the damp air was filled with laughter and joy.

There are tears at times, of course. But Camp Good Mourning was a happy place that day, filled with almost 100 kids from the Atlanta area who had lost a parent or sibling. They had come to camp to face grief together through Kate's Club.

Kate's Club is an Atlanta-based nonprofit created in 2003 by Kate Atwood, who, at 12 in 1991, lost her mom to breast cancer. Its purpose is to support bereaved kids ages 5 to 18 by bringing them together with their peers for weekend outings, grief support through art and music therapy, and its signature programmatic event, Camp Good Mourning. The annual two-day camp, which took place at Camp Twin Lakes in Rutledge, Georgia, was designed to connect grieving kids in a camp setting to activities, friendship, and solutions for managing their grief in healthy and positive ways.

I had joined the Kate's Club Board of Directors in June 2011. Whenever I pitched Kate's Club to potential donors, Bryan's story was always the one I told, rather than my own. My service to the organization and its mission was driven by the wish that a Kate's

Club had existed in Columbia to support my younger brother during the four years after our dad's suicide.

But today wasn't for fundraising. Today was for fishing, with pancakes as bait; for climbing a two-story-high pole, pushing through terror in order to leap and grab a trapeze; and for attacking the zip line and the elevated swing.

"My stomach, like, dropped!" Grace giggled about the swing. "It's really fun!"

This is Kate's Club.

Kids are given the space to laugh, and cry, and grieve. One moment they're giggling, the next they might need support, and in the blink of an eye they're reciprocating for a brother or sister in need, biological or otherwise.

The Luminary Walk is a signature element of Camp Good Mourning that had always had an impact on Mary, my fellow board member (and future board chair). This year, Mary said, she had been surprised the night before to see her cabin of girls as composed as they were. But the composure hadn't lasted very long because just as with the death of a parent or sibling, everything can change in a split second.

"About 20 seconds later I felt silent sobs wracking the body of one of my campers, who was walking in front of me, and then came a low, long wail," Mary recalled, noting that these tears gave the other girls permission to not be OK. "The rest of the cabin—except for one camper walking with her little sister—dissolved into tears."

"We made it back to our luminaries and just sat," Mary said. "The little sister went back to her luminary a couple of cabins down, and the big sister then had her release. She didn't want to cry in front of her sister—a brave 10-year-old protecting her six-year-old sister. Last year's walk was emotional, but this year's was more raw and deep."

Kate's Club had my whole heart during the five years I spent there volunteering. I connected with adults and kids who lost a parent like I had, and I learned about grief, compassion, friendship, and nonprofit leadership from the excellent staff, dedicated board members, selfless volunteers, and resilient kids. I also gained deep insight into my own grief journey, and how it intertwined with my ongoing battle with anxiety, depression, and suicidal ideation.

My time with Kate's Club provided almost endless opportunities to gain perspective—about the wreckage that death can leave in its wake for the people touched or shattered by that loss, and about the humanity of invested adults who want to ensure that children and teens know they aren't alone on their grief journey.

I learned that when we experience the trauma of losing a loved one, our traumatic event isn't a variable throughout our lives. People wonder why we don't "get over it." But, in reality, our trauma is forever a constant, frozen in time. We are the variable, and as we grow and age, we re-experience our traumatic event or events as we move through the stages of our lives.

At best, we gain perspective. At worst, we melt into a puddle of fear, pain, tears, and exhaustion. But once we understand that *we* are the variable, we can then realize that we're not broken because we can't "get over it."

We're simply human.

October 16, 2000

GETTING THE STORY isn't always as simple as scheduling interviews.

Successful journalists often need a bit of luck. And on this Monday in Washington, DC, as I wandered across the National Mall from the Lincoln Memorial to the Washington Monument and United States Capitol, it seemed like divine intervention was the only chance I'd have to successfully tell the story assigned to me by my editor.

I loved covering sports but wanted to explore the news side of journalism. So, several months earlier, I'd deliberately moved from sports to the news desk, because I wanted to have secured a non-sports reporting job by the time I graduated on December 19.

I'd agreed to an unpaid internship on the "other" side of the newsroom at *The State,* but with one request—I wanted to spend my fall break in Washington. My ultimate career goal at this juncture was to live in Washington and write for *The Washington Post* by the time I was 30.

I was still 22, and I was on assignment in Washington. My job today was to cover the South Carolina angle of the Million Family March, which had been coordinated by the Nation of Islam to celebrate family unity and racial and religious harmony. This march was being held on the fifth anniversary of the Million Man March, which had aimed to bring visibility of Black issues back to prominence in the national conversation following the 1994 Republican Revolution. This electoral pushback against Democratic President Bill Clinton's "liberal agenda" had seen conservatives gain 54 seats in the US House of Representatives and eight seats in the Senate, to control both bodies.

I had a cell phone, but my contact with the Nation of Islam's Columbia group had declined to give me his cell phone number, telling me "If we were meant to meet in DC, then we would meet." Audrey was my photographer for the day, so she and I walked around the Mall, searching for fellow South Carolinians. Luckily, painted signs giving a Palmetto State-shout-out helped us find a group from home.

It was reassuring that my inability to find whom I was looking for was apparently a shared experience. "I've been gone for about two hours trying to find my brother," said Linda, a Loris, South Carolina native. "It's a great feeling, greeting people from different states. It's just wonderful."

Linda's positive perspective, and the fact that I'd found at least one South Carolinian to interview, helped quell my anxiety as Audrey and I walked around the Washington Monument a little later, wondering what to do next. That's when I saw him.

"Earl!" I called out to the man I'd met at the Nation of Islam meeting in Columbia a few weeks earlier. He smiled in a told-you-so kind of way as I approached.

"It's going along just as planned," he told me about the march. "We got to know each other on the bus, but the real test comes when we get back home. Maybe we can start a dialogue and come together to work out all of the differences for the human family."

These two interviews (along with another conversation, this time with a group from Columbia's Benedict College that I'd run into) meant that, through some good luck, I had enough material for my first Washington-based news story.

I spent my next two days with Michelle, *The State*'s Washington reporter, who was working out of Knight-Ridder's Washington bureau. She had the perfect blend of talent, knowledge, and patience to take a very green 22-year-old news reporter under her wing and answer all of my seemingly endless questions.

Michelle treated me to lunch at the National Press Club, where she was covering a news conference, before taking me to meet 97-year-old Sen. Strom Thurmond at his Capitol Hill office. Then she let me assist with a campaign finance story and graciously included my byline with hers. She's a gem, and gave me an excellent crash course in political reporting during our time together.

But the most critical meeting of this trip had come at a sports bar in Virginia days earlier, where Audrey and I met up with Fred—my high school sports editor from *The State*—and his friend Alan, also a USC graduate and a former reporter at *The State*. Fred had moved north only weeks earlier to join the sports staff at *The Washington Post*. Alan was writing for *Education Week*, a national magazine that covers K–12 education issues. We were all USC fans, so we were meeting to watch the Gamecocks play Arkansas. We had fun watching Carolina win its sixth football game of the season, which was six times as many as the one win we'd had in the prior two seasons combined when we'd gone 1–21 during my first two football seasons at USC.

My anxiety over finding the right newspaper job by graduation led me to focus as much on seeking career advice as watching the game. Alan kindly offered to meet me for lunch later in the week to talk more about my job search before I headed back to Columbia. I took him up on it, and we met at Austin Grill near Bethesda, Maryland, where *Ed Week* was headquartered.

During that first of many future lunches with Alan, he told me about his first post-USC newspaper job, which was at the *Herald-Journal* in Spartanburg, a decent circulation-size daily newspaper. Alan raved about his experience there. I noted mentally that

Spartanburg was only a 90-minute drive from Columbia, where Audrey would still be at USC for another 18 months.

When I returned home, I quickly reached out to the *Herald-Journal* to see if they had any openings where I might be a fit following graduation. They were hiring for reporting positions in their bureaus in the cities of Greer and Union, so I sent in my resume, letters of recommendation from multiple editors at *The State*, and clips in a package.

I also asked my mentors to call editors at the *Herald-Journal* to talk me up. Fred, Alan, and Ernie, my faculty adviser at USC, all made calls on my behalf. Soon after that, Bob, the *Herald-Journal*'s city editor, called and invited me to come to Spartanburg to interview for one of the bureau jobs. While I was there, he told me a business writing job was also available in their main newsroom.

I knew very little about business journalism in the traditional sense, so I told Bob that I'd prefer a news job but would be thrilled to join his paper in any capacity.

Four days before my December 19 graduation from USC, my journalism luck hit its peak: when Chris—the *Herald-Journal*'s 25-year-old rising-star business editor, former sportswriter, and fellow USC graduate—called to offer me the business writing job. I couldn't say yes fast enough.

I was finally about to be a full-time professional newspaper journalist.

July 15, 2008

NOT ONLY WAS today my first Election Day as a campaign worker, but I'd technically made it in *The Washington Post* at 30 years old.

My goal was to be a reporter at *The Post* and that didn't happen, but there I was, standing behind Congressman John Lewis in the picture that accompanied the story about his first contested Democratic primary election since 1992.

After my transformative experience meeting Congressman Lewis in Alabama roughly three years earlier when I was a reporter covering the 2005 Congressional Civil Rights Pilgrimage, I had pledged to myself that I'd volunteer for Mr. Lewis the first time he drew a campaign challenge.

In the Spring of 2008, he was facing two challengers—and so, in May, I walked into his campaign office on Northside Drive, a block from the Georgia Dome, to offer any help I could give. I'd stuff envelopes, make yard signs, call voters, or anything else that was needed in support of this American hero.

Running Involvement through News and Civics (Inc), the small nonprofit I'd started three years earlier, wasn't taking all of my time, so I was able to volunteer in Democratic politics, first through Young

Democrats of Atlanta (YDAtl), and now on the congressman's primary campaign.

Tharon, our campaign manager, gave me the priceless opportunity to support Andrew, the press secretary, on communications-related work, along with whatever else was needed each week.

My favorite day of the campaign is captured in that photo, which ran with *The Post*'s election day story about "Obama Generation" candidates challenging longtime leaders like Congressman Lewis. We'd spent that June Saturday morning and early afternoon knocking on doors in the Cascade neighborhood in Southwest Atlanta.

Knocking on doors in congressional races for longtime incumbents wasn't typical, especially in contests that weren't likely to be close. But John Lewis, although a five-term incumbent, wasn't a typical candidate. He wanted to work harder than his opponents, and he wanted to talk to the people he represented. So, off we went, the Congressman plus a team of 12 clad in blue "John Lewis for Congress" T-shirts, who were determined to earn permission from voters to put signs in their yards after Mr. Lewis asked for their vote.

While walking with the Congressman, we came upon a man mowing his yard. Before we knew it, Mr. Lewis was giving the man a breather and mowing the yard himself, in the process earning both a yard sign placement and a legendary story for his team to share in perpetuity. The moment was captured by a photographer, and when this story ran on July 15 in *The Washington Post*, there I was in the background, barely visible behind the Congressman as he mowed.

"I'm going to be fine," Congressman Lewis correctly predicted in *The Post*'s Election Day article. "I've been working very hard."

When I tell the story about that day, the Congressman cutting a constituent's grass is where I always start. But that episode was actually only the second-best part of the day.

The best part happened at lunch, while I did some mowing of my own, devouring an order of J. R. Crickets' spicy, citrusy Fester wings (a mix of lemon pepper seasoning and buffalo sauce now known as

"Lemon Pepper Wet" after a 2016 shout-out on Donald Glover's *Atlanta*). While he treated his team of staff and volunteers to lunch, Congressman Lewis shared story after story from his experiences in the Civil Rights Movement. I sat across from him for more than an hour, in awe as he shared memories about the people of the movement whom he'd fought alongside. They hadn't become household names, but in his opinion, they were the essential foundation of the movement's success.

Two months earlier, on April 24, I'd heard another, more specific set of stories while I sat across from him in his Capitol Hill office in DC to conduct a video interview, which would be shared during YDAtl's "Future is Blue" event as part of a reflection of 1968's 40th anniversary. This conversation with the Congressman was another pinch-me moment, as we talked specifically about the two-month period in 1968 that began on April 4 with the murder of Martin Luther King, Jr., and ended on June 6 with the assassination of Robert Kennedy.

In 1968, Mr. Lewis—then 28—was working on Robert Kennedy's presidential campaign, advising on issues of racial injustice, and he was there in Indianapolis on Thursday, April 4, when Kennedy delivered the news of King's murder to a predominantly Black crowd at a rally that Lewis had planned for that evening.

"What we need in the United States is not division; what we need in the United States is not hatred; what we need in the United States is not violence and lawlessness, but is love, and wisdom, and compassion toward one another, and a feeling of justice toward those who still suffer within our country," Kennedy told the crowd that night.

Mr. Lewis was also in California on the night that Kennedy was shot after winning the California Democratic primary.

"Sometimes when I'm sitting on the House floor or in a committee meeting, or speaking someplace, I often think, 'What would Martin Luther King, Jr. say? What would Robert Kennedy say?

What would Martin Luther King, Jr. do? What would Robert Kennedy do?'," he told me that day in his office.

My role on Primary Election Night was to monitor results as they rolled in; my YDAtl friend Megan and I chose a table at the election party to set up a laptop to track numbers. We answered endless questions about the evolving numbers until it was clear that the Congressman had defeated his primary challengers—which he did with 69 percent of the 5th District's votes.

The 5th District was the real winner that night, but it was quite a feeling to have worked on my first political campaign—for an American hero—and to have made it into *The Post* in a picture with him.

I couldn't have scripted a better way to kick off my thirties.

May 10, 1999

THE ANNOUNCEMENT THAT *Rent* was heading to Broadway came on Friday February 23, 1996.

Early on February 24, my dad ended his life.

Between that date and this one, I'd started a long-term relationship, graduated high school, left home for college, finished two years at the University of Alabama, ended the relationship, transferred home to USC, secured my first professional journalism job at *The State*, and finished my junior year in college.

But through all of that, I'd been in a haze—sleepwalking, essentially.

Then I walked into the Nederlander Theater on West 41st Street and made my way to the balcony, along with my roommate Jason and our fraternity brother, Mike. We were road-tripping from Columbia to Baltimore (to pick up Mike), then to New York (only my second visit), finally on to Boston, and then back.

I'd been in charge of choosing a show for us to see, and all I knew as we settled into our seats was that *Rent* was supposedly still the musical to see in 1999 if you were going to experience Broadway. I didn't know the story—that this "rock opera" was a modernized version of Giacomo Puccini's *La bohème*. (In fact, I didn't know of Puccini, *La bohème*, or really even opera itself, for that matter.)

I also didn't know the backstory of Jonathan Larson, who didn't live to see the show that he'd created find its way to Broadway or receive worldwide acclaim. (He'd died alone on the kitchen floor of his Greenwich Street loft from an aortic aneurysm, just hours after *Rent*'s first dress rehearsal on January 24, 1996.) And I definitely had no idea that Larson's masterpiece would awaken my heart and transform my soul.

Rent is about living in the moment. It's about embracing love as love. It's about overcoming isolation to achieve connection. It's about experiencing the fear that comes with living life while awaiting death.

In *Rent*, Larson swapped 1830s Paris for New York's East Village in 1989. He Americanized character names and occupations. And he substituted AIDS for tuberculosis as the deadly illness stealing young lives.

The grief journey following the death of a loved one is typically long, winding, and ever evolving.

I had been progressing in my grief journey for the three years since Dad's suicide, but what happened in that theater was personally revolutionary. Feeling the show's music, the stories, and the *emotions* as they pounded through my mind, chest, and soul gave me the perspective I desperately needed to begin to lift myself out of my emotional stupor by helping me realize that life is a gift.

Because we never know how much longer we have.

So, we must live it. Experience it. Own it.

Engage.

Laugh.

Talk.

Love.

Connect.

Do all the things we can while we have time because time is not something we control.

These principles are revelatory and, in some contexts, revolutionary. *Rent* helped me see the world anew.

I was raised in a white, apolitical, middle class family that lived on the "nice side of town," 20 minutes from downtown Columbia—where, at the same moment in 1999 that we were experiencing *Rent*, the Confederate flag was still flying from the dome of the South Carolina State House.

On that day in New York, I wasn't liberal or conservative. I was disconnected and sheltered by privilege. I was a mindless zombie to the realities of the world around me.

I'd witnessed my share of racism throughout my 21 years, but was too much of a coward to call it out, even though that was my inclination. I had been unintentionally complicit because I had been thoughtlessly ignorant. But that day changed me.

I don't believe you can love *Rent* and hate other people.

It opened my eyes to homelessness.

It opened my eyes to AIDS.

It opened my eyes to the LGBTQIA+ community.

It opened my eyes to love and identity in all forms.

With open eyes, I realized that the most important things to me were civil and human rights, and equity for all people.

Rent has been transformative for countless people since it opened in 1996. Some love the music. Some love the characters and the story. Some love how it opened their eyes to the world. And some, like me, love it for each of these reasons and more.

What *Rent* taught me is that if a choice exists between love and hate, there is no choice. Love wins. It knows no bounds. And it's right. Always.

Rent's final song, "Seasons of Love," asks us how we'll measure the 525,600 minutes that define a year. It gives us examples. But what were my examples?

Who was I? How would I measure a year?

In movies? In bylines? In road trips? In games of baseball?

However we each choose to measure a year in our fleeting existence, *Rent* teaches us to do so through actions that reflect respect for every human life.

This is a lofty standard, and our own fear, pain, damage, and insecurities can get in the way of showing that respect, even when we have the best intentions. At times, I have failed this test, but no longer because I'm a zombie or uninformed—but because I'm human myself.

Between May 10, 1999, and October 15, 2000, I visited the Nederlander on four separate occasions to see four *Rent* casts from four different vantage points (including Standing Room Only) to experience and re-experience those life-changing 140 minutes.

I've probably listened to the original cast soundtrack more than 525,600 times.

The premise of the song "What You Own" revolves around longing for true connection at a time when our technology isolates us from each other more and more. This message is illustrative of my struggle with anxiety and depression, and maybe yours.

After all, it's human connection we all crave in some form. Just as the lyrics of "La Vie Bohème" taught me that creation, rather than peace, is the opposite of war, I've learned in Alcoholics Anonymous that the opposite of addiction isn't sobriety, but connection.

For this alcoholic, it is deep loneliness and lack of connection that takes my mind to its darkest moments of suicidal ideation. I also believe that to truly soak up every one of the 525,600 minutes we get each year, we must treat all humans with respect, dignity, and love as we work to connect with them.

We must be kind.

We must be present.

We must be intentional.

We must speak out against injustice.

We must be active in changing the flaws in the world and in ourselves, and we must push through our dark moments to stay alive, so we find the connection we seek and spare our loved ones from lifelong disconnection from us.

Ultimately, if we successfully do these things, we will truly be able to measure our lives in love.

July 25, 1994

WHAT THE FUCK just happened?

Wasn't I just sitting on a dock with a beautiful girl?

No, we'd already left the lake house.

So, why was I looking at the sky?

Why did my head hurt?

I ran my hand through the left side of my swoopy brown hair, and it came back covered in blood. Our wreck came flooding back to me as I jumped up in terror to look for Sara.

I'd been thrown from her red Chevrolet Cavalier, and was desperate to find this seemingly flawless human whom I'd met only several weeks before. As I ran to the car, I couldn't see her, but I could hear her crying from the back seat. She was alive, thank the Lord. I couldn't find any blood, but she was in pain. I helped her get out. We sat on the ground beside her car's undriveable carcass, held each other, and cried.

We were in the middle of nowhere—a few miles from her grandparents' lake house on Lake Wateree, nearly 30 minutes away from her house in Winnsboro—and 45 minutes from our unplanned next destination, Richland Memorial Hospital in downtown Columbia.

We'd only been dating for a couple of weeks. And we hadn't known each other for a month yet, after meeting on July 1 in a church van with a handful of other teens heading to North Greenville College for a Christian camp called Centrifuge.

I'd never believed in love at first sight until I stepped into that van. Meeting the gaze of Sara's mesmerizing royal blue eyes and feeling the warmth emanating from her lovely smile, I became a convert.

Twenty-four hours before that, I hadn't intended to go on that trip. But my buddy Jamie had signed up and convinced me to call our youth pastor to see if I could snag a spot. Fortunately, there'd been one. Since I'd only planned to watch baseball, play Sega, and go to the pool that weekend, I'd agreed to tag along.

Sara was there as the guest of a member of our youth group with whom she played tennis, but very quickly I was convinced we were there to meet each other.

Now, 24 days after meeting, we had cheated death together. We sat in shock by her crushed convertible—in which, two weeks before, I'd leaned in and met her lips for our first kiss.

The next part is blurry. EMTs arrived, loaded us in the ambulance, and jammed in our IVs. Then, off we went to Columbia on a romantic trip to the emergency room. As sirens wailed and the ambulance sped along, we clasped hands as we laid on our gurneys throughout a rough drive that seemed far more frightening than the wreck itself.

As we laid there in silence, it started to come back to me.

She was driving. I was slightly reclined in the passenger's seat. The convertible top was closed, and I wasn't wearing a seatbelt. The right front wheel skidded off the road at some point between the lake house and the main highway. She overcorrected, and the car went out of control, rolling a couple of times before landing on its wheels, parallel to the road.

As it was happening, I screamed, "This is just like my wreck!" Five months before, on February 22, I'd been driving my gray 1987 Honda Accord to see USC play The Citadel in baseball at Sarge Frye

Field with a couple of baseball teammates and had had the same kind of accident.

My right front wheel had gone off the right side of the road. I'd overcorrected. We'd rolled a couple of times and landed on the driver's side. Luckily, both my friends and I had come away from that wreck relatively unscathed. I'd been told at the time that I was alive only because I had been wearing a seatbelt.

On this humid July Monday with Sara, I was probably alive because I hadn't worn one. When I found her in the back seat, I saw that the right side of her windshield had been crushed from the rolling. Had I been in the front passenger seat, it would have been far worse for me than the injuries I received from being thrown out of the car.

I ended up with a separated left shoulder and a gash on the left side of my head. Sara had broken ribs, one of which had punctured her kidney. But we were both alive.

On our second date, we'd seen *Speed*. Near the end of the film, there was a prescient line that we laughed about after our wreck. "I have to warn you, I've heard relationships based on intense experiences never work," Keanu Reeves's Jack had told Sandra Bullock's Annie.

At that moment, we weren't worried about that. We were happy to be alive. So much so that four days later, on Friday, July 29, we drove past the scene of our accident and returned to the dock on Lake Wateree, where the sweetest memory of our first month together came as she and I sat beside each other, reflecting on our near-death experience.

On that dock, Sara told me about kindred spirits—people we immediately connect with on a deeper level. A definition of kindred spirit that I love is that it is someone who "from the very first moment you meet, you have a feeling they understand everything about you, and you them."

We were both only 16, but I believed I had found my person. Our connection had been clear on July 1, our first couple of weeks dating had been dreamlike, our wreck had been a nightmare, but now we were back on this dock, lucky to be alive, and telling each other "I love you" for the first time.

It was an ethereal memory to balance the traumatic ones we'd created only four days before.

I have lots of memories from June 1994. My first trip to New York City. My hero Ryne Sandberg's abrupt retirement from the Cubs. The video of Lisa Loeb's "Stay" playing every hour on MTV. Watching Pedro, Puck, and their roommates on *The Real World: San Francisco*. The national coverage of the murders of Nicole Brown Simpson and Ron Goldman. O.J. Simpson's subsequent Bronco chase on the 405 freeway in Los Angeles being shown live in a box on the screen during NBC's coverage of Game 5 of the NBA finals between the New York Knicks and Houston Rockets.

But, from July 1994, I only remember Sara.

October 15, 2015

I SAT ON THE dusty, enclosed dock at Camp Twin Lakes among people I had only met hours before. All I could do was nervously grip, flip, and catch the Milwaukee Brewers-branded baseball I'd found in a box a couple of months earlier, after I'd moved to my new apartment in Atlanta's Old Fourth Ward.

The get-to-know-you assignment for this leadership retreat was to bring a sentimental personal object that was illustrative of a key episode in our personal story. My divorce wouldn't be final for two more weeks, and it hadn't yet hit me how much my life would change after being married for the previous 13 years.

Now, even on a dock full of potential new friends, I felt more alone than I'd been since before Audrey and I started dating in July 2000, and I was about to open up to this group of strangers about the ground zero of my abandonment issues.

After we returned to Columbia on February 19, 1996, from my college visit to Tuscaloosa, Dad had gone on a business trip to Milwaukee. When he returned that Friday, his final full day on earth, he'd given me this blue and green baseball with Brewers branding embossed on its cowhide covering.

Maybe it was an attempt to connect, but it was probably just a final, parting gift in advance of the two-page, typed letter I would receive the next morning, which would chisel his final words into my terminally impacted psyche.

Other than the time that Audrey and I had witnessed a particularly embarrassing Braves loss at Miller Park in 2004 while we ate juicy bratwursts drenched in spicy mustard, I had zero connection to the Milwaukee Brewers, other than this ball. Baseball was such a part of my life, so a ball from his final trip made sense, and it was logical for me to share this item and tell my new friends the story of my dad's suicide.

Additionally, I was navigating an emotional untethering from divorce as the paperwork that would officially end our 13-year union would be signed by a judge in the next two weeks. Audrey was a wonderful woman and partner in so many ways, but we'd been on divergent paths since we moved to Atlanta in 2006. While she'd become immersed in building a litigation career at one of the world's largest law firms, I'd first been paralyzed for 18 months by my anxiety and depression, and then had been mostly absent as I invested all my time in finding a foothold in the dual Atlanta worlds of Democratic politics and young professional leadership networking and climbing.

Those two worlds had pushed my "prove myself" buttons and in no time, I'd been mainly concerned with winning campaigns, building my network, and achieving award-based recognition opportunities. This had all been great for my resume but had done very little to satisfy the craving for the approval that, in my mind, I never had been able to receive from my dad.

Audrey and I had always talked about having children, and in 2008 had even bought a five-bedroom home, which in my mind indicated that starting a family wasn't far off. But then, while we were back home in Columbia in 2009 for Thanksgiving, she'd shared with me that she had changed her mind, and no longer wanted kids.

The story I told myself was that because of my dad, my DNA, and my damage, she simply didn't want to have children with *me*.

We had already been growing apart, and for the next couple of years, I'd consciously chosen to just not bring up having a family. Instead, I'd pledged to myself that I'd try to be a better person and husband, so that maybe she'd change her mind again.

Whether or not I'd be a good father is certainly up for debate, but the day of my dad's suicide, in addition to the promise I'd made to myself to talk about the things in my head, I'd also committed to being the best dad I could be, if ever I had the great fortune to have a family someday.

In 2014, after Papa died, my heart was broken, my meds weren't working, I was actively thinking about suicide, and I'd fully bought my own story that Audrey didn't value me and had decided that I'd be a bad father. In reality, maybe it wasn't about me at all—but she gave me no insight, so my anxious mind created its own narrative.

The fact that we wouldn't be having children brought into focus all the irreconcilable aspects of our marriage. We'd turned into roommates and ships passing in the night. I loved her and valued her, but any emotional intimacy we'd shared had disappeared long ago.

In February 2015, while on a solo trip to New York to observe the 19th anniversary of Dad's death, I'd finally come to the realization that our marriage was over. We wanted different things, and in June, shortly after our 13th wedding anniversary, I told her there wasn't a path forward together.

Audrey definitely deserved better than I was able to give, and I'd come to believe that the ideal situation in life for me was a partnership that was fulfilling for both people. The second-best option was being single and happy. And the worst choice was being in a relationship that wasn't fulfilling for either partner, which is where we were after 15 years.

Starting over at 37 wouldn't prove to be easy. Despite not consistently giving me the emotional intimacy I desired, my marriage had given me a depth of emotional security of which I wasn't fully aware. Even if I had understood that fact, divorce was still the best path.

Single and happy, however, was far easier said than done. The deep abandonment issues gestating inside my mind had been kept at bay by marriage. Now they were rapidly manifesting in emotional and destructive ways as my trust issues began to play out in ways I'd never have predicted.

But right now, on this chilly, clear Thursday morning, at the same camp where Kate's Club hosted Camp Good Mourning annually, I decided to not be shy about telling my story and putting all my daddy trauma and abandonment issues on the table before this new group.

As it worked out, I'd find some lifelong friends during our experiences together in the coming months of our seven-month-long leadership class. But, as my post-divorce nerves continued to fray, I was barely able to be present and maximize this wonderful opportunity to enhance and strengthen my individual leadership skills. And what I was going to need professionally more than anything in 2016 and 2017 was the ability to be a stable leader.

Had I been able to predict the inevitable emotional chaos I would experience post-marriage, maybe I would have been able to prepare myself and deal with life as a single person in a healthier fashion. Instead, I drowned my fears, anxieties, and insecurities in bourbon and whiskey, becoming increasingly toxic to others in my personal and professional lives.

And I faced off against more consistent suicidal ideation than I'd experienced in my life, thinking more and more about the ways for me to die. I'd ended my marriage. Why not end my life?

February 13, 2007

I'D HAD VERY, very few panic attacks while Audrey and I were living in South Bend during her three years at Notre Dame Law. From March 2002 through May 2006, the Paxil that I'd been prescribed was intended to restore the balance of serotonin in my brain, and it seemed to work.

But for some reason, when we moved back to the South in May 2006, I'd already convinced myself that all my mental health problems would cease when we settled into our new city, Atlanta. So, without medical advice, I'd decided to eliminate the Paxil from my daily routine and bloodstream. A debilitating nine months had followed.

I had chosen to start my life in Atlanta with no journalism job, no meds, and no real friends.

The isolation resulting from this combination led to a state of anxiety and depression the likes of which I'd never experienced. I'd finally given up on trying to do it myself, and so, on this day, I was going to return to therapy for the first time in years.

My experiences in therapy to this point had been unproductive. I'd never been able to build trust with a therapist the way I believed was needed to create positive change for myself. But I couldn't continue to live the way I'd been living, inside my head. I knew I needed therapy, and I knew I needed to get back on meds.

Researching options through our health insurance, I'd found a female psychologist who specialized in trauma and anxiety issues. I am far more comfortable talking to women, and over the course of my life I'd had more close friendships with them than I'd ever had with men. I've always been sensitive and connected to my emotions, but grew up in a world where guys didn't talk about such things with each other.

Today, as I made myself comfortable on Dr. Spring's couch, I gave a big speech about how I'd never been successful in therapy, and how, if I were going to be, I needed her to push me from the beginning—because left to my own devices, I'd build an emotional wall that would make our sessions ineffective. And so, we began our work together.

My anxiety and depression had been fueling my need for control; over the previous nine months, I'd had far too much and far too little control, all at the same time.

On one hand, I could do anything I wanted. I was starting a non-profit, Involvement through News and Civics (Inc), and was trying to figure out exactly how to do this new job without experience, confidence, or compensation. I was theoretically in control. I just didn't have a clue what to do.

Inc was created to provide free newspaper subscriptions to lower income families while helping to get them more involved in their community through our Family Reading Initiative.

In partnership with my former employer, the *Herald-Journal*, we'd been piloting this program with a group of families in Spartan-burg, which is about a two-and-a-half-hour drive northwest from Atlanta. So, every month or so, I'd escape from my self-made jail to travel back to my old stomping grounds to inch the nonprofit forward programmatically while working from Atlanta to fundraise and build organizational infrastructure in collaboration with our board, which was made up of college and professional friends of mine who all lived in cities spread out across the country.

Inc had talented and dedicated board members like Chris, my former business editor; my college roommate, Brandon; Jeff and Lilly, whom I met while covering Habitat for Humanity during my time at the *South Bend Tribune*; and my college friend Jeanette, who was now an up-and-coming public relations whiz.

But none of them were in Atlanta and, in any event, I wasn't brave enough to share my mental health struggles with any of them because I wanted to project confidence as our nascent nonprofit's day-to-day leader.

In total, this was a far-from-ideal situation to be the basis for personal or professional success. I was essentially alone on a daily basis. And my non-medicated mind was not at all in control. While Audrey billed countless hours as a rookie litigator at her law firm, I stayed home with our dog Sandberg, DVDs, and reality TV, struggling mentally and professionally.

As a journalist, my work positioned me to meet people organically. I only knew how to build relationships through this paradigm. Left to my own devices, my social anxiety kept me from even investigating how to meet other people.

So I didn't.

I wouldn't find a friend in Atlanta who wasn't a coworker or friend of Audrey's for several more months, when I reconnected in May with Alan, the journalist I'd met in DC back in 2000. He'd moved to Atlanta around the same time Audrey and I had, but it took a year for us to reconnect.

Over lunch, I invited Alan to be Inc's first Atlanta board member. Then, not long after, I reconnected through Facebook with Alcide, an old middle school classmate from Columbia and now a talented lawyer. He became Inc's second Atlanta board member and a trusted friend.

These two specific reconnections ended up being lifesaving for me, personally and professionally. But these friendships might not have been possible without finding my way to Dr. Spring. From the beginning, she fostered an environment in which I was able to find mental stability for the first time. I was now seeing Dr. Spring every two weeks, and I was back on meds for anxiety and depression, thanks to the psychiatrist she recommended.

I was beginning to rebuild myself after nine months of emotional paralysis. With that psychological foundation in place, I could engage with other humans in Atlanta, rather than hide at home with my blind yellow lab and my movie collection. And with Atlanta-based collaborators in Alan and Alcide, I'd renewed relationships with indispensable old friends and essential new allies to establish Inc in Atlanta.

As a result, I was able to rediscover my confidence and find my place in the Atlanta nonprofit, political, and young professional communities.

September 26, 2009

O UR TEAM OF seven had 15 minutes to discuss the project we'd been assigned before the nonprofit's executive director would arrive to tell us all about her organization.

We'd only met the day before, as part of a group of 42 young leaders from Atlanta—all between 26 and 32 years old—convening at Berry College's WinShape Retreat near Rome, Georgia to begin our city's premier young professional leadership program.

At 31, I was deeply intimidated by my classmates, who were lawyers and doctors and CEOs. They'd earned degrees from Harvard and Morehouse and Emory. Many had JDs, MBAs, or master's degrees and some even had multiple post-graduate diplomas.

Odette was an on-air reporter for WABE. Tharon was running a mayoral campaign. Catherine was a senior aide to Atlanta Mayor Shirley Franklin. Mandy was the Director of Sustainability for the City of Atlanta. And Steve, who was now a lawyer representing youthful offenders in appellate cases, had pitched for Clemson in the College World Series and been drafted by the Colorado Rockies—and those last two things weren't even in his bio. I only had my little old bachelor's degree in journalism from USC and the tiny nonprofit I'd started.

My social anxiety was doing its best work to make me feel less than worthy of inclusion. It told me I had more to prove than was possible. But, deprecating self-talk aside, I was deeply grateful to meet and be in the company of new peers, and to have been selected for this talented and diverse class of Atlanta's young leaders.

As part of our year-long leadership experience, each class member was placed on a team of seven and paired with a local nonprofit to work on a social impact project. My jaw dropped slightly as I read the description of the organization our team would be working to support: VOX Teen Communications, an after-school program that had been founded in 1993 as a teen newspaper for the Atlanta area.

Teen journalism! Seriously? I couldn't have been paired with a more ideal nonprofit to put my experiences, talents, and passions to work in service of a mission.

Then, a burst of energy blasted through the door, modeling the culture of the organization she'd created alongside teen leaders in 1993, when she'd been just 23 years old.

To me, Rachel was immediately the most impressive, compelling, and exciting young leader at our retreat. Her passion for VOX's work and her commitment to teen voices were absolutely infectious.

Her "go around" question led our group into an amusing game of Two Truths and a Lie. Then, after Rachel's warmth and get-to-know-you exercise melted the ice away from these buttoned-up young leaders, she explained to us that VOX wanted to create an earned-income stream—kind of like how cookies bring in money for the Girl Scouts—by leveraging VOX's organizational assets: teen voices, a top-notch adult staff and board of directors, and long-standing partnerships with media companies such as *The Atlanta Journal-Constitution* and Turner Broadcasting.

After Rachel oriented us to the project, we were left to pick a liaison to VOX from our team and brainstorm our project.

Other than founding Inc, stepping up as a leader wasn't part of my story. But when I saw the description of VOX, I felt like the universe had divinely placed me in this specific group, to work on this specific project. To me, this was a sign that maybe I should volunteer for a leadership role.

So I raised my hand.

I couldn't have known it in that moment, but this seemingly small choice would turn out to have the greatest impact on the direction of the nonprofit part of my career since I had decided to leave journalism when we moved to Atlanta in 2006 to focus my time and energy on launching Inc.

July 17, 2000

OUR SUNDAY FLIGHT from Boston had been canceled because of weather, so now we were flying back to South Carolina on Monday afternoon.

Being late always triggered my anxiety, racing heartbeat, and sweat glands, but this was worse.

I was supposed to pick up Audrey for our second date at 7 p.m., and being on time was looking dicey. We'd had a good time on our blind date a week earlier, so we'd made plans to go out again tonight.

I'd already purchased and changed into a dark blue long-sleeve, button-up shirt from Brooks Brothers at Boston Logan International Airport because I likely wouldn't have time to do anything but get from the airport to my house, jump in my car, and drive 30 minutes to pick Audrey up from her parents' house on Lake Murray.

I had been on assignment for *The Post and Courier* to write about Charleston, South Carolina native and Gamecocks shortstop Drew Meyer, who was playing in the Cape Cod League. The year before, I'd spent time with Drew and his family in Charleston as part of my high school baseball coverage for *The State*. He was the top high school player in South Carolina in 1999 and was deciding between joining the Los Angeles Dodgers (who had drafted him) or coming to play at USC for the Gamecocks, which he ultimately did.

During the flight, all I could think about to quell my pre-second-date anxiety was the fun trip we'd had over the past few days. Mom and Bryan had joined me for this short-but-enjoyable family vacation weekend in and around Boston. I'd introduced them to Fenway Park—where we watched future Hall of Famer Pedro Martinez strike out 10 Mets—before spending a couple of days on Cape Cod. There, we ate "lobstah," and watched Drew's Chatham Athletics in action as he honed his wooden-bat skills in the premier college summer league.

The Cape's towns and villages are rabid for their teams, and they turn out in droves for the games even though they feature a new cast of characters each summer. "It's a really friendly atmosphere," Drew had told me. "It's like a town get-together. It's really nice how they put it on."

We finally landed in Columbia, and I arrived on time with her knowing nothing of my anxiety.

It turned out she was still getting ready and as I waited for her in her parents living room, I could only laugh at myself for being exceedingly anxious about being on time.

November 23, 1996

WHEN RUNNING BACK Dennis Riddle scored from six yards out with only seconds left to lift Alabama to a 24–23 Iron Bowl victory over Auburn at Legion Field in Birmingham, I was on the bus in the parking lot with my Sigma Chi pledge brothers. We missed the end of the final regular season game of Gene Stallings's legendary coaching career because, as pledges in 1996, we did what we were told, and we were told to head to the bus.

Days later, I wrecked my six-month-old 1996 Saturn SC-2 and had to fly back to Columbia for Thanksgiving with dirty clothes filling my two bags because I hadn't learned to do my own laundry. Fortunately for the people around me during my first semester of college, Mom washed my clothes every third week, when I made the six-hour drive each way from Tuscaloosa to Columbia and back.

But I wasn't going home that often for laundry. I was going home to see my family. I was going home to see my girlfriend, who was still in high school at Spring Valley (she'd graduate in May 1997 and join me at Alabama the following fall). And I was going home to try to escape from the nagging idea that I was only at my dream school because of the money that came to my mom from my dad's life insurance after his suicide.

"I want you to go to the college of your choice," Dad had written early in his suicide letter to me. "I also want you to apply yourself and enjoy yourself at the same time."

On this Alabama football Saturday night, it was nine months to the day since my final conversation with Dad. I'd arrived in Tuscaloosa on August 16, and these had been the most difficult three months of my life for many, many reasons. Primarily, I had no idea how to process Dad's suicide and handle my own grief, but on top of that, pledgeship had been extremely difficult. We were never physically hazed, but pledging was a nonstop endeavor, every single day.

Each morning, we'd arrived at the fraternity house by 8 a.m. for breakfast and stayed there all day until dinner. There were two exceptions, the first of which was going to class. I was also granted brief reprieves from my life as a Sigma Chi pledge whenever I was on assignment for *The Crimson White*'s sports section, including writing a story on the three-headed-monster running back group of Riddle, Curtis Alexander, and star freshman Shaun Alexander.

The second was when a brother directed us to complete a task; these might be simple errands, rides to class, cleaning around the house, or quizzes on our knowledge of fraternity history and/or member facts. After dinner each night, we'd had study hall until 9 p.m., and then we'd headed home—or to a pledge party with sorority pledges.

Greek life at Alabama is famously a way of life, but it wasn't ever something I'd considered before my first visit to Tuscaloosa. Dad, Mom, Bryan, and I had made the trip along I-20 west from Columbia on Presidents' Day weekend for my college visit. I'd been accepted to Alabama the previous December, and I wanted to visit campus before I made my decision.

I'd fallen in love with the school immediately. It was everything I pictured when I thought of a college campus in the South: a massive, grassy quad with a library (Gorgas Library) at one end and a bell tower (Denny Chimes) at the other, and red brick classroom buildings with white trim lining its right and left sides; as well as the massive football stadium (Bryant-Denny) a block away.

Beyond the appeal of this setting, UA offered me a journalism school that was one of the best in the Southeast, and a legendary football team to watch and support. One of my key stops that weekend had been to visit *The Crimson White* to learn as much as I could about how to become a reporter there if I were to attend. When I walked in that Saturday, I'd met Scott, the Administrative Affairs editor, who told me all about the student paper and what to expect as a freshman reporter.

His T-shirt had Greek letters on the front pocket, so I'd figured I'd ask about his fraternity as part of our conversation. I didn't drink and I had no idea what to expect from fraternity life, but Scott seemed like a good guy. He'd asked me for my phone number and address, and said he'd put me on their list in case I wanted to come to a rush party in the summer.

This had all seemed so foreign to me, especially the simple idea of accepting an invite to a party, but I'd figured nothing would come from it anyway. Then, two months after Dad died, I'd received a letter in the mail, inviting me to Tuscaloosa in June for Sigma Chi's largest summer rush party.

Not long after the letter arrived, I'd called Scott to tell him about Dad's death, and that I'd decided to attend Alabama in August, but I wouldn't be able to make the party in June.

Scott shared his condolences, and then made me promise to let them know when I was coming for Orientation. This way, he could introduce me to some of the guys in the fraternity.

In July, I did just that, and the night of my orientation, I found myself in a back room of a two-story house on 13th Street with a handful of guys around me asking me if I would accept a bid to be a Fall '96 pledge. I gratefully accepted and flew back to Columbia with my pledge pin fastened to the inside of my pants pocket for safe keeping.

My only instruction for fraternity next steps was after I had moved into my dorm, I was supposed to head over to the fraternity house. On August 16, after Mom, Bryan, Wally, Pam, Gina, and Abby had left me in my dorm room in Paty Hall, I'd had a good cry. I'd never been as uncertain or scared, but I knew this was where I needed to be because it was the last thing Dad knew. My anger toward him had only grown in the six months since his death, but I needed to prove that I could thrive in this new world I was insistent on joining in the days between my college visit and his suicide.

I composed myself, put on a brave face, and headed to the Sigma Chi house to meet a few of my pledge brothers and start this new life. Outside of baseball teammates, I'd never had the opportunity to have a group of male friends like this before.

They were all pretty great guys. Most of us had very little idea of what was in store for us, but one of my first friends, Brian, was a sophomore, and he filled us in on what he knew from spending his freshman year outside of the Greek system.

A couple of weeks later, it had already become clear that my dorm roommate and I weren't a good match, so I'd moved to a windowless room in Brian's off-campus house. This became a respite from pledgeship stress, not only for the two of us, but for everyone in our pledge class.

By the time I flew back to Tuscaloosa after Thanksgiving break, pledgeship was winding down ahead of finals. Those of us who "made grades"—a minimum 2.5 GPA—would be initiated after we returned from Christmas break in January. We were at the point now where the most difficult parts of pledgeship were behind us: there were no more early Saturday morning cleanups after Friday night band parties, no more football games where we'd have to wear suits and bring dates and hold seats, and no more Sunday night pledge meetings.

There was only the promise of initiation, wearing Sigma Chi T-shirts as actual members of the fraternity, eating meals without being quizzed, and attending chapter meetings.

After a week of initiation tasks and silence, Brian and I (and the other eight of our pledge class who had cleared the 2.5-GPA academic threshold) were initiated on January 11, 1997. This group of guys had been my only support system in Tuscaloosa as I navigated life away from home and without a father. I tried to open up as best as I could, but didn't know how to let others help.

As the first anniversary of Dad's suicide approached, I'd accomplished one of my life's most difficult achievements to date—fraternity initiation. I wish I'd done it without all the drives home that kept me from building stronger connections with my new friends. But I did what I needed to do to survive in the world without the daily presence of my family.

In the process, I learned a lot about myself. I learned what having a group of guy friends was like. And less importantly, I learned how to mop. I learned to always carry a pen. And I learned that if you're on time, you're late. I also learned that if I opened myself up to others, there was a chance that I could find my place in the world, and it didn't have to be in isolation.

Sadly, that last realization would be no match for my own grieving, anxious, fear-driven mind.

November 21, 2009

I'M NOT SURE how many plates of debris fries our crew made disappear while we watched Ole Miss upset LSU (ranked No. 8 at that moment) in football, but the bill was longer than a CVS receipt, pretty evenly split between alcohol and debris fries. Debris fries are French fries that are covered in leftover roast beef, tossed in brown gravy, then smothered with melted shredded cheddar cheese, and finally, topped with biting, intense horseradish sauce.

In New Orleans, a city filled with unforgettable food, they're a standout.

We were there to celebrate Brandon, my college roommate and a key founding member of the Inc board. His wedding was set for early the following year; our group had descended upon the Big Easy for his bachelor party, which was built around food, alcohol, and college football. The small group of Brandon's groomsmen were mainly Sigma Chis from our USC years; they had pledged the fall of 1996, as I had at Alabama, and had been wonderfully welcoming to me when I transferred to USC in 1998. I'd always felt fortunate to connect with them back then, and now we were reconvening nine years after graduation.

I'd never had as much to drink as I'd already had that weekend, and this was only day two. I'd started drinking Friday morning on the plane with a screwdriver, and literally had only stopped to sleep. Fortunately, I'd remained mostly in control because I spaced out my liquor drinks. Alcohol always washed away my anxiety. I was happy and having a blast.

I'd first been to New Orleans in 1996, when my Sigma Chi pledge class traveled from Tuscaloosa for our pledge retreat. That's when I bought The Tabasco Cookbook, from which I still make Eula Mae's jambalaya every month or so; its sauce-stained pages show the love and the wear of 25 years. Then I'd been back with a group of Young Democrat friends to celebrate after the 2008 election.

In April 2014, I'd follow up this weekend by embarking on a wall-to-wall food adventure with Audrey. We'd eat for three straight days, hitting Commander's Palace, Cochon, La Petite Grocery, Café du Monde, Central Grocery, and Galatoire's. We'd even drive 137 miles west to Avery Island for a Tabasco factory tour. But for me, New Orleans is about far more than Tabasco and beignets and jazz and muffulettas and po' boys.

New Orleans holds a tremendous amount of importance in our family history. It was where Papa began his ministry after earning his degree from New Orleans Baptist Theological Seminary on January 17, 1958. He then moved his family almost 400 miles northeast to Moulton, Alabama, where he pastored his first church, and where the harrowing story we heard as kids took place.

In the late 1950s, a white Southern Baptist preacher wasn't looked on kindly for supporting civil rights in Alabama, and Papa's engagement with Black Christians certainly wasn't tolerated.

So Papa was sent a fiery message.

The Ku Klux Klan erected a cross in front of the modest Riley home, hung a gasoline-filled tire on each arm, and set the cross ablaze. The house had a long front yard that led to the street, and, as an adult, my mom—who was 10 at the time—told us that she could close her eyes and still see that cross burning.

"Papa slept with a handgun under the mattress for a while," she recalled. "It was a scary time."

Even while focused on nonstop food and drink, I couldn't visit New Orleans without remembering it as the place where Papa had found his spiritual voice and commitment to all humans during seminary.

When I think of him, I always think about the twin stories of fire and ice, remembering that burning cross in Alabama and his frozen feet in Belgium.

Stories like these established him as the hero in my life.

Ultimately, Papa was the only man who never let me down, and his approach to life provided me with a roadmap to serve others as he and Bee had done for so many years in their churches, in their communities, and in our family.

March 4, 2005

"**T**HREE MINUTES."

The ominous whisper on the other end of the phone had been life saving for Carolyn, but not for the four little girls she had just been speaking to in the bathroom, where they died at the hands of white supremacists on Sunday, September 15, 1963.

"Bombing in Birmingham was a way of life," Carolyn told the visitors to 16th Street Baptist Church. There, Addie Mae Collins, Cynthia Wesley, Carole Robertson, and Carol Denise McNair were murdered. The explosion that killed them was created by an incendiary device planted by four members of the Ku Klux Klan. These men had attached 19 sticks of dynamite to a timer and hidden it beneath the steps on the church's east side.

It had been almost 42 years since 14-year-old Carolyn answered that call, as she recalled the terrorism that took place on that dark day. That's why I was back in Alabama for the weekend. To remember. To reflect. To share. To learn.

The Congressional Civil Rights Pilgrimage had begun in 1998, when Congressman John Lewis, a Black Atlanta Democrat, and Congressman Amo Houghton, a white New York Republican from Corning, led 10 other members of Congress on a bipartisan weekend in Alabama.

There they had walked through civil rights history: in Birmingham on Friday, and in Montgomery on Saturday, before remembering Bloody Sunday in Selma during the annual Sunday march across the Edmund Pettus Bridge. That bridge was where, on March 7, 1965, the 25-year-old Lewis, along with Hosea Williams, Amelia Boynton, Bob Mants, Albert Turner, and more than 500 other Black marchers, had been attacked and brutally beaten by Alabama state troopers and a posse of deputized white men, while marching for voting rights for Black Americans.

"It's like going to Normandy with Dwight Eisenhower," Congressman Houghton had told the Rev. Doug Tanner, founder of the Faith & Politics Institute, which sponsored the annual pilgrimage, to be led by Lewis until his death in 2020.

On this day in March 2005, I'd traveled from South Bend, Indiana to cover the three-day remembrance that would culminate, on the 40th Anniversary of Bloody Sunday, with the march in Selma from Brown AME Chapel and across the Edmund Pettus Bridge.

Why would a reporter for the Michigan bureau of the *South Bend Tribune* need to be in Alabama for this weekend?

Luckily for me, the congressman I covered, Republican Fred Upton of St. Joseph, Michigan, had paid for three teens from his district to join him and experience this weekend with Mr. Lewis and Civil Rights luminaries like Coretta Scott King, the Rev. Joseph Lowery, and the Rev. C. T. Vivian. My managing editor, a student of the Civil Rights Movement, had quickly approved my travel request so that I could capture the stories of the weekend through the experiences and words of those Michigan boys—Cash, John, and Ardale.

Little did I know how this assignment would change my life. Not only would it open my eyes to a movement I'd only read about, but it would allow me to meet an American hero who would ultimately have a massive impact on my life.

Before that weekend, my list of heroes had included my maternal grandparents, Bee and Papa Riley, and Ryne Sandberg, the Cubs second baseman, who would be inducted into the Baseball Hall of Fame four months later, in July 2005. But by the time I flew back to Indiana from Atlanta that Sunday night, Congressman John Lewis would join that short list of heroes.

Mr. Lewis was a hero to so many Americans long before I met him, and he would inspire countless more in the next 15 years—even following his death on July 17, 2020 from pancreatic cancer.

On that Friday, I shook his hand for the first time and interviewed him as we stood in the sanctuary of 16th Street Baptist.

Congressman Lewis told me that recounting civil rights memories "over and over again" for teens like Cash, John, and Ardale would impact future generations and continue to change our country for the better. "Maybe by telling this story, people will remember and never forget," he told me that Friday in Birmingham. "And maybe what happened here will never again happen in America."

Hearing from the people who had personally experienced the 16th Street Baptist Church bombing, only a handful of feet away from where it happened, gave new perspective to Cash, 17: "It opened my eyes to how segregated it was, and how white folks despised the color of our skin," Cash told me. "It made me appreciate more that our African American leaders planted the seeds for us."

The next morning, we all were together again in another sanctuary, this one 90 miles south in Montgomery at Dexter Avenue Baptist—the church Martin Luther King, Jr. co-pastored from 1954 through 1960 with his father, "Daddy" King.

John, 15, had never heard these stories before. He'd learned about Rosa Parks's refusal to leave her seat and move to the back of the bus, but hadn't been taught about the Montgomery bus boycott, which started four days after her act of nonviolent protest and lasted for more than a year, from December 5, 1955 to December 20, 1956.

"It's just not what we've learned in school," he said as he wrote in his blue-and-gold journal. "There's tons more. When I write, I take myself out of right now, rewind, and closely look at what I've seen."

What Cash and Ardale (who are Black and grew up in Benton Harbor) and John (who is white and grew up in St. Joseph) experienced up close were the same race issues present between their "twin" cities, which sit in Berrien County along Lake Michigan in their state's southwest corner. In 2005, Benton Harbor, with a population of about 10,000, was approximately 90 percent Black, while across the St. Joseph River in St. Joseph, about 88 percent of its 8,400 residents were white.

Whirlpool Corporation, founded by the Upton family, is headquartered in Benton Harbor and is one of the largest employers in the area, bringing white-collar executives from St. Joseph and blue-collar workers from Benton Harbor.

In June 2003, a month before Audrey and I moved from Spartanburg to South Bend for her to start law school at Notre Dame, Benton Harbor had been engulfed in two days of protests—called riots by national news outlets—in the wake of the death of Terrance Shurn, a Black man who had crashed his motorcycle into a building and died following a chase by local police.

Alex Kotlowitz's 1998 book, *The Other Side of the River*, investigates the two cities as a "living metaphor" for America's racial divisions. He tells this story through the mysterious death of Eric McGinnis, a Black 16-year-old from Benton Harbor whose body was found in the St. Joseph River on May 22, 1991, three days after he disappeared.

Now Cash, John, and Ardale—who were growing up experiencing very different childhoods on opposite sides of the St. Joseph River—were traveling together to experience civil rights history through the essential places and people of the movement. "This has impacted me more than I'd expected," John told me, as we sat in what's now known as Dexter Avenue King Memorial Baptist Church.

On Sunday, we took our reflections from the past two days about 50 miles west of Montgomery, to the packed pews of Brown Chapel AME Church in Selma.

Over the previous two days, we'd experienced Birmingham and Montgomery in the midst of a few dozen people, of whom Congressman Lewis was the most notable national figure.

Today would be quite a contrast. This was already becoming apparent, as some people were allowed to join the service inside Brown Chapel while hundreds more would wait outside for the march to step off for the half-mile through downtown Selma to the base of the Edmund Pettus Bridge.

Inside, during the three-hour service, the Michigan teens and I would hear from such luminaries as Coretta Scott King, the Rev. C. T. Vivian, the Rev. Jesse Jackson, and, of course, Congressman Lewis.

"We didn't become bitter," Lewis remembered, during his speech. "We didn't become hostile."

They fought with nonviolence then, and they continued that fight 40 years later.

"The issue is not Black or white," the Rev. Vivian said during his remarks. "It's justice or injustice."

When small wicker baskets were passed from person to person to collect an offering for the church, Ardale didn't hesitate: "I see what they need it for," he whispered to me, as he slipped a few dollars into our basket. "I'd love to see this church stay around for a lot more years."

Moments later, we were all marching through downtown Selma in solemn memory of the fortitude of organizers and marchers who had walked these same streets 40 years before as they set out to traverse the 54-mile US Route 80—then known as Jefferson Davis Highway, after the former president of the Confederacy—between Selma and the state capitol in Montgomery, as part of the fight to secure full, unimpeded voting rights for Black Americans.

The 1965 march was organized by Amelia Boynton and James Bevel, who were working with Dr. King at the Southern Christian Leadership Conference (SCLC) in the wake of the murder of

Jimmie Lee Jackson on February 26, 1965. The SCLC, where Dr. King was president until his assassination in 1968, would coordinate the march with the Student Nonviolent Coordinating Committee (SNCC), where Lewis was Chairman. A founding SNCC member, Lewis was lovingly known as "the boy from Troy," per King's description of him based on his Alabama hometown, which sits about 85 miles southeast of Selma.

In 1965, when SNCC's Lewis, SCLC's Williams, and the marchers behind them reached the other side of the bridge and crossed into Dallas County, Alabama, state troopers and the posse of "deputized" white men were lined up with billy clubs and tear gas, waiting.

A famous *Life* magazine cover photo under the words "The Savage Season Begins" captured the face-off in its final moments before the racist, violent chaos at the hands of uniformed white men and their angry, plain-clothed peers erupted.

When the dust settled, Lewis's skull was cracked and bleeding from a billy club's direct hit, Boynton's throat was burned from the gas that had been pumped into her eyes and mouth by an officer standing over her unconscious body, and 15 other marchers also had to be hospitalized.

But their pain and sacrifice would awaken large swaths of the country, which were now watching more than ever as violent racism played out on the nightly news, in the morning papers, and on the covers of weekly magazines. This awareness led to a shift in public opinion that helped to ensure the passage of the Voting Rights Act of 1965, which President Lyndon Johnson signed on August 6, 1965.

"I often think about, 'What if they had given up?'," Ardale told me after we had all crossed the bridge together safely. "Where would we be? People in the past worked so hard for what's given to us, so we should take advantage."

From Alabama that weekend, I sent a story back each day to South Bend for the *Tribune* to share with its readers. The stories were told through the eyes of Cash, John, and Ardale, alongside the memories and insights of American heroes like Congressman Lewis and the Rev. Vivian. Like these teens with whom I'd experienced the Alabama trip, I'd never received this education either. Moving forward, I'd seek it out. Through books, conversations, and experiences, I'd continue to learn and grow and try to contribute to a more just America and world.

When I returned to South Bend, I told Audrey—who had already accepted a summer associate offer in the Atlanta office of a global law firm—all about my weekend. We agreed that, after we moved to Atlanta in May 2006, we would always live in Congressman Lewis's district and support him in all the ways we could.

That commitment would prove to be life changing.

January 10, 2000

T HE NEW CENTURY was beginning, and I was finding the courage to speak out against racism.

This wasn't the typical thing done by white Southern fraternity boys at the time, but in the past six months, my eyes were finally beginning to be opened to the realities of the ignorance that had swirled around me, mostly unnoticed, for more than two decades.

Fighting back against injustice should be automatic, but unfortunately, that's often not the case. As we put the uneventful Y2K in the rearview mirror, I was starting to seize opportunities to learn more about racism, speak up, and act out against it.

For the first time, I'd penned an opinion column after I agreed to write the "liberal" side of a point-counterpoint in today's issue of *The Gamecock*. I had opposed my co-Sports Editor regarding the racist, homophobic, and xenophobic comments made by Atlanta Braves closer John Rocker in the December 27, 1999, issue of *Sports Illustrated*.

Two weeks earlier, my roommate Jason and I had been shooting pool at Jillian's, a few blocks away from the South Carolina State House, when Rocker's comments to the magazine about whether he would ever play for either New York team were plastered across ESPN on the big-screen TVs.

"I'd retire first," Rocker had told *SI.* "It's the most hectic, nerve-wracking city. Imagine having to take the [Number] 7 Train to the ballpark, looking like you're [riding through] Beirut next to some kid with purple hair next to some queer with AIDS right next to some dude who just got out of jail for the fourth time right next to some 20-year-old mom with four kids. It's depressing." He continued: "The biggest thing I don't like about New York are [*sic*] the foreigners. I'm not a very big fan of foreigners. You can walk an entire block in Times Square and not hear anybody speaking English. Asians and Koreans and Vietnamese and Indians and Russians and Spanish people and everything up there. How the hell did they get in this country?"

Rocker earned a two-week suspension from Major League Baseball for his comments, but went on to pitch in another 89 games for the Braves in 2000 and 2001 followed by 70 more games for three more MLB teams from 2001 to 2003.

My colleague's counterpoint boiled down to the age-old shell game of hiding behind the First Amendment. I argued that no one had said Rocker should have been jailed by the government, but a private company can basically fire an employee for any reason, whether they've reflected poorly on the company's brand or because of their performance. Few complain when pitchers are garbage on the mound and they lose their opportunity to pitch. I argued this was no different.

"Baseball is a game," I wrote in my conclusion for *The Gamecock* column. "Games are meant to be fun and games are meant to entertain. Games are not meant to give ignorant people platforms to offend as many people as possible."

Then, a week later, I was presented with another opportunity to speak out against injustice, this time in person.

It had been 135 years since the end of the Civil War, but the Confederate flag was still flying from the mast atop the dome of the State House in downtown Columbia—blocks away from the USC campus—despite increasing pressure for it to finally come down.

Even though I grew up in the state that was the first to secede from the Union, the Civil War, the horrors of slavery and racism, in general, weren't really discussed in my family. I never heard anything overtly racist from anyone in my immediate or extended family, but we also never discussed the contemporary realities of racism in Columbia, in the South, or in America. It was as if it was something that happened long ago, rather than the living, breathing, insidious reality pervasive across our city, country, and world.

My whip-smart and deeply progressive friend Rachel, a fellow journalist at *The Gamecock*, had been an incredibly positive influence on me where social justice was concerned. She asked questions I'd never been asked and engaged me in conversations that were long overdue. She simultaneously scared and inspired me. On Sunday, January 17, after a trip to see *Girl, Interrupted*, she invited me to join her the next morning in a march to protest the flying of the Confederate flag atop our state capitol.

Earlier in the month, a pro-flag rally at the State House had drawn around 6,000 people from the heritage-not-hate crowd, but on this day, Rachel and I were among a much larger group—estimated at 46,000 people—as we marched the half-mile from Zion Baptist Church on Washington Street to the capitol at Main and Gervais Streets. James T. McLawhorn, president and CEO of the Columbia Urban League, told *The State* at the time that it "was the largest gathering for social justice" in South Carolina history.

I'd never been in the midst of anything like it. Crowds weren't my favorite, in general, but the energy of the mostly Black marchers permeated my soul as the lyrics of Civil Rights-era protest anthems wafted through the air and my mind. My anxiety was replaced with love, light, and an entirely new insight into the idea of community. (Each year since that January 2000 march, "King Day at the Dome" has grown and is now a must-attend for political candidates and elected officials to actively observe Martin Luther King, Jr.'s legacy on the holiday bearing his name.)

Four months later, on May 19, 2000, the South Carolina Legislature would finally vote to remove the flag from the top of the Dome; it would be ordered by Democratic Gov. Jim Hodges to finally come down on July 1, 2000.

While gone from the dome, the Confederate flag would continue to fly on the capitol grounds until July 10, 2015, following the June 17 murders of nine Black church members, including State Sen. Clementa Pickney, during bible study at Emanuel AME Church in Charleston by a 21-year-old white supremacist with a Glock handgun.

On the day of the Charleston murders, I would be the executive director for VOX Teen Communications, where we supported teens from across the Atlanta area as they worked to find, hone, and share their voices through journalism and self-expression.

Along with my experience seeing *Rent* in May 1999, writing that column for *The Gamecock* and marching on MLK Day in 2000 would help me to evolve, opening my eyes to forms of injustice that I'd never been aware of up to that point in my life. Then, 15 years later, hearing first-person reflections and insights from Atlanta's Black teens would have more impact on me than all the marches, protests, reading, and conversations I'd experienced by then in my 37 years.

Even with all the perspective gained up to and through my time at VOX, I would make mistakes in my role as executive director and learned a lot about how to be a better ally through my missteps.

Leadership failures like these would trigger guilt and shame, which, for me, would lead quickly to worthlessness and, in turn, thoughts of ending my life.

It's easy to fall into the habit of catastrophizing our failures, large or small, and make them an excuse to end things. But we don't have to do that. The only way to be a better ally and human being is to listen to feedback from others, learn from our mistakes, and keep marching forward.

But this is only possible if we stay alive.

For me, that means not only having an ongoing commitment to life, but also to a healthy relationship with humility that sustains me during continuous reflection. To achieve this I have to listen, work to be a better version of myself, and consistently strive for social justice: through my words, and, most importantly, through actions that align with those words.

June 23, 2005

I'D BEEN PLANNING for this week for more than a year, but I never could have prepared for the impact on my life that getting to know families receiving newly built homes during the 2005 Jimmy Carter Work Project would have.

Habitat for Humanity International annually rotated its signature home-building event between domestic and international locations. In April 2004, former president Jimmy Carter went to Benton Harbor to announce that the 2005 build would focus on Michigan, with 225 homes to be built across the state, including 20 in Benton Harbor and 30 in Detroit.

One of the key reasons that I'd been able to convince my *South Bend Tribune* bosses to let me spend a full week covering this transformative event was because I'd been selected by Whirlpool Corporation as one of two local journalists to have their own private, one-on-one interview with President Carter during the five-day build. Whirlpool, based in Benton Harbor, was Habitat's largest corporate partner at the time, providing every Habitat home built across the world with a range and refrigerator.

President Carter, along with his wife, Rosalynn, had begun building with Habitat as volunteers in 1984. He loved to build, but said what he loved the most was the ownership each new homeowner exuded when they received their key after their home was ready.

"When they build their own house, they're very proud of what the product is," our 39th president told me, while he took a break from helping a family build their new home.

Six Habitat homes were also being built in Windsor, Ontario, across the Detroit River in Canada. Today, as part of my week-long coverage of the build, I'd traveled to Detroit to write a story on Whirlpool volunteers from Benton Harbor.

I reflected on the week while driving from Detroit to Windsor with my friend Jeff, who led the Habitat partnership for Whirlpool. We'd become fast friends during my coverage over the past year, despite the fact that he was a graduate of Clemson University, the more historically successful team in the Tigers-Gamecocks sports rivalry.

During my coverage that week I'd met dozens of new homeowners, who were some of the most wonderful people I'd met in my life. They included Roxie, who found lifelong friendships with the volunteers as she worked alongside them, turning a concrete slab into the first home she'd owned.

"I wish this was still nothing but concrete," she'd told me. "Then, I could do it all again."

Roxie and others had also told me something I couldn't shake from my mind. During the week, I'd heard from many of the families that they didn't read the newspaper often because they couldn't afford it. Sometimes, they'd borrow a neighbor's Sunday paper on Tuesday, or they'd go to the library to read the paper if they needed to know something.

But the price was the barrier.

As we rode in a van to Windsor, I told Jeff that I wanted to do something to change this. Financial barriers shouldn't exist between people and public information, an idea that ultimately would end my journalism career in May 2006 as I began the process a week later to create a nonprofit designed to provide newspaper subscriptions to low-income families.

Meeting so many extraordinary people in connection with that week of coverage caused a total paradigm shift in my definition of community. I'd always wanted to be safely in the background, covering the work of others, sharing their stories with the world. But I couldn't unsee the hands, hearts, and infectious smiles of everyone involved in that week's build, from Jimmy and Rosalynn Carter to the new homeowning families, to volunteers and Habitat employees.

Our new nonprofit—ultimately named Involvement through News and Civics—found two of its first, crucial board members that week: Jeff, my friend from Whirlpool, and Lilly, the astute and lovely volunteer coordinator for Harbor Habitat, Benton Harbor's Habitat affiliate. Thanks to Whirlpool, my Habitat coverage was reprinted in a special section of the *South Bend Tribune* that included a column I wrote to reflect on the week.

"I'm fairly convinced that I didn't truly understand the concept of giving until I spent a week with Habitat for Humanity volunteers," I admitted in my first-person musing. "What I found was this ideal microcosm of society where all that mattered was the creation of sustainable change. Race didn't matter. Neither did socioeconomic status nor political leanings nor educational background. Everyone worked toward a common goal that was accomplished within an exhilarating, life-changing week."

June 6, 2013

A S THEY SAT in the second row of the theater at Atlantic Station, the teenagers had no idea what was about to happen.

They knew that we were all there to preview the new zombie flick *World War Z*. This was thanks to Rich, our talented and well-connected editor, who always secured exclusive opportunities for VOX teens to cover entertainment stories like film previews. But we'd kept the best part a secret.

When the door opened, shrieks echoed across the theater as Brad Pitt walked in, high fived the VOX teens in the second row, and gave a quick introduction to *his* film, which they were about to experience.

He was as gone as fast as he'd arrived, off to do the same thing at screenings in other cities. But during his cameo, he'd left a lasting impression.

"He. Touched. My. Arm!" rising senior Vaughn reminded us throughout the rest of the day.

Around this time a year earlier, I had been interviewing with hopes of becoming VOX's executive director. The interview process had been both exhausting and invigorating. Ultimately, I'd finished second to a nonprofit executive from New York who had more nonprofit experience than I offered.

I'd been heartbroken when Todd, VOX's board chair, met me for coffee to give me the news. Nonetheless, the interview process had helped me craft my own personal narrative and in the process, made me realize that I needed to be working where I was passionate about and invested in the mission. For the remainder of 2012 I'd mixed political and nonprofit contract work, hoping to position myself to earn the right full-time job when it arrived.

On January 2, 2013, the call that I'd dreamed of receiving in July 2012 had suddenly come out of left field. VOX's new executive director hadn't worked out, and they wanted to know if I was still available and interested in discussing the position.

When I originally applied for VOX's executive director job, I'd referred to it as my dream job during the interview process. This wasn't just a line—I meant it with every fiber of my being.

I'd been a teen journalist and a professional journalist. I'd started Inc, which was still operating. And I'd spent eight months, from September 2009 through April 2010, working on our nonprofit impact project at VOX with my team from our young professional leadership class. During our project, I experienced VOX's truly special culture while getting to know its dynamic founder, Rachel, members of the board of directors, and a few VOX teen leaders. For all these reasons, I was personally invested in VOX's mission and embraced its "teens first" culture. It was my ideal next professional move because I wanted to lead a nonprofit where I loved the work and was invested in the mission and constituents.

Following that surprising call on January 2, I met with members of the hiring committee to discuss the job, talked to my friend and VOX board member Whitney, called Rachel to make sure she was supportive of my hire, and as quickly as I could, I accepted this life-changing opportunity.

VOX is voice in Latin. The nonprofit's core operating principle is that all teens and adults involved with the organization exist on a level playing field. Facilitating teen voices and leadership is therefore the expected approach of every VOX adult, whether staff, board member, volunteer editor, or writing coach. Seats on the board of directors are reserved for teens, and they are involved in hiring, strategic planning, and almost all other significant decisions.

During the school year, teens spent time between 4 and 7 p.m. daily at VOX's downtown newsroom to work on content creation with Rich and program planning with Katie, our dedicated and skilled program director. Katie and Rich expanded on Rachel's legacy each day, creating a safe space for teens to not only create content and lead, but to share and grow and explore with adults treating them as peers. Then on Saturdays, teens returned weekly for programming and fellowship. Every day at VOX is a blast thanks to everyone's commitment to embrace and expand the culture Rachel built with countless Atlanta teens since 1993.

But nothing compares to the summer, when teens are at VOX all day, Monday through Friday, participating as summer interns or as participants in VOX Media Café (VMC), a hands-on-opportunity for teens to explore multimedia techniques for storytelling, while learning the fundamentals of journalism and creating a tangible multimedia product with Atlanta's top media professionals. VMC had been developed, in part, from our young professional team's idea of creating a summer camp as VOX's new income stream for the final deliverable of our nonprofit impact project.

Even though I was having a blast in my new job as VOX's executive director, as I approached my six-month anniversary, my anxiety and self-doubt were catching up fast.

Imposter syndrome was beginning to overwhelm me daily, and I was spending far too much of my time trying to prove that I belonged in the role. I'd had smaller leadership opportunities before VOX, and although I'd been a risky choice on paper because of my absence of experience running an established nonprofit, I was doing a good job so far.

But that factual reality was nothing my anxiety and insecurity couldn't ultimately crush if I weren't vigilant—and I wasn't.

My management style was to try and meet people where they were and manage the person's approaches and abilities; my leadership philosophy was to fill whatever role needed to be filled, rather than being the center of attention at all times. But, as I began to doubt myself, I questioned my worthiness of this incredible opportunity.

I had the best of intentions, and as much passion as I'd had for any job. But did I have the emotional wherewithal to be the leader that VOX teens and adults needed on a daily basis? Or was I just the kid with the all the potential that still only made Cs?

I was hearing my dad in my ear, telling me that anything less than perfection wasn't enough.

"Commit yourself to excellence, so that you will feel proud of your efforts and accomplishments," Dad had written in his suicide letter to me. "If you only get by, you will rob yourself of the joy of success for your hard work."

I believed that his advice was reasonable and, taken at face value, could have been used for good. But I was unable to take it at face value. It had come to me at the expense of his life, and of any future we might have had in which I could have asked him follow-up questions, or for guidance when I was stuck, or lost, or in desperate need of course correction.

I was beginning to question my value to this place that I loved deeply, and to tell myself that VOX had been right when it didn't hire me the first time. My incessant self-doubt and daily insecurity would ultimately be a self-fulfilling prophecy as I simultaneously grew and regressed personally and professionally in the coming years.

November 4, 2008

TODAY WOULD HAVE been Dad's 60th birthday.

Though we'd never talked about politics, I'm almost certain he would have been voting for Arizona Sen. John McCain, like most Southern white men his age.

Me, not so much. Like so many Americans, I had been captivated by the vision, ideas, and oratory prowess of Illinois Senator Barack Obama.

He'd already gained my support and vote before he earned the Democratic nomination, and today, he received my vote again. For the past year, I'd dedicated most of my free time to the Young Democrats of Atlanta (YDAtl). I'd wanted to be involved politically after I moved to Atlanta and left journalism, but my social anxiety would never have allowed me to just show up at Manuel's Tavern on Highland Avenue on the first Wednesday night of the month, knowing no one, for a YDAtl meeting.

Luckily, the universe intervened, as it often does.

In October 2007, Involvement through News and Civics (Inc), the nonprofit I'd started in 2005, had hosted its first Atlanta fundraising event at SweetWater Brewery to support our Family Reading Initiative. My dear friend and most dedicated Inc board member, Alan, had invited some of his coworkers. A group that included

Aaron, the kind, affable, and thoughtful YDAtl membership chair, who had then invited several of his YDAtl friends.

While talking in SweetWater's tasting room, Aaron had encouraged me to join him on November 7 for YDAtl's next meeting. That opening, and Alan's willingness to come, had led me through the doors of legendary Manuel's Tavern for the first time to put myself out there to this new political world.

After diving in headfirst to anything YDAtl would let me do in early 2008, I'd been invited by Mijha, YDAtl's brilliant Wellesley- and Yale Law-educated president (like Hillary, she'd tell you) to join YDAtl's executive committee as communications chair. It was the first time since I left journalism that I'd felt valued by others. That acceptance had helped launch a journey that would become a defining part of my life for the next decade.

This past June, I'd taken over as campaigns chair for the rest of the year. In that role, I'd coordinated all of YDAtl's volunteering with state and federal campaigns, including the US Senate race in which beloved former State Rep. Jim Martin was running against Sen. Saxby Chambliss, the incumbent Republican.

Now, it was Election Day. We had knocked on doors together, phone banked together, watched the debates together, and eaten many, many Manuel's meals together.

Tonight, almost a year after my first YDAtl meeting, we were together at the Hyatt Regency on Peachtree Street for the Democratic Party of Georgia's election night celebration. We'd started the night upstairs in a suite where the Red Clay Democrats were hosting their young professional members when Obama officially won California—and the election—shortly after 11 p.m.

We cheered, hugged, and then sprinted downstairs to ensure that we were in the ballroom in time for Obama's acceptance speech.

It would literally be in the final minute of November 4 that our first Black president would begin speaking to the crowd of more than 125,000 that had begun gathering in Chicago's Grant Park hours earlier to celebrate everyone from Martin Luther King Jr. to Rosa Parks, to Congressman John Lewis and countless more Black Americans who had in some way contributed to this hard-fought and long-overdue victory—and to the many millions of viewers across the US and around the world. I didn't see a dry eye amongst my YDAtl friends with whom I had the privilege of sharing this moment.

"This victory alone is not the change we seek—it is only the chance for us to make that change," our newly elected president told us all. "That cannot happen if we go back to the way things were. It cannot happen without you. This election had many firsts and many stories that will be told for generations, but one that's on my mind tonight is about a woman who cast her ballot in Atlanta."

The room erupted when he mentioned our city.

"She's a lot like the millions of others who stood in line to make their voice heard in this election except for one thing: Ann Nixon Cooper is 106 years old," President-Elect Obama said. "She was born just a generation past slavery; a time when there were no cars on the road or planes in the sky; when someone like her couldn't vote for two reasons—because she was a woman and because of the color of her skin. And tonight, I think about all that she's seen throughout her century in America—the heartache and the hope; the struggle and the progress; the times we were told that we can't, and the people who pressed on with that American creed. Yes, we can."

We were ready to answer the call to action by our new president as we stood arm-in-arm in that ballroom.

"America, we have come so far," he told us and the world. "We have seen so much. But there is so much more to do. So tonight, let us ask ourselves—if our children should live to see the next century; if my daughters should be so lucky to live as long as Ann Nixon Cooper, what change will they see? What progress will we have made? This is our chance to answer that call. This is our moment."

When we walked to find our cars and head home around 2 a.m., all we could hear was the cheering, honking, and screaming echoing up and down Peachtree Street in downtown Atlanta.

It was no longer Dad's birthday, but I was convinced this was the birth of better days for America.

November 7, 2017

THROUGH MY NEED to people-please, my inability to say no, and my extreme anxiety about money, I had overcommitted myself to almost a dozen candidates or projects for Five Points Civic Strategies, the consulting business I'd started in late 2016. But, through all the juggling, drinking, and chaos of 2017, there was one goal that mattered to me more than the others.

We had to get Amir elected to the Atlanta City Council.

That quest had begun during the summer of 2008, when I first met Amir at a YDAtl Happy Hour at Front Page News in Atlanta's Little Five Points area. I'd recently finished my first-ever campaign, volunteering for Congressman John Lewis's primary race. Amir had told me he was running for Atlanta City Council, and after talking a few more times, he'd invited me to volunteer as he began his campaign for an at-large citywide council seat.

By June 2009, volunteering had turned into my first paid campaign role as Amir's Outreach Director. This job combined the responsibilities of communications, direct voter contact at doors and through phones, volunteer management, and planning meet-and-greets that were to be hosted by supporters so their friends and neighbors could meet Amir in person.

It had been a crash course in all things campaign, and despite Amir's runoff loss on December 1, 2009, the experience built the foundation on which I would establish myself as a successful political campaign operative in the coming years.

Since 2010, Amir, Howard, and I—at times together and other times in separate pairs—had discussed Amir's follow-up run to his 2009 race. Then, in 2016, Amir had decided that he would run to represent Atlanta's District 2 on the City Council. The seat was open because its incumbent was vacating the seat. Ultimately, Amir would have four opponents and, with Georgia's election rules, he would face another December runoff unless he could exceed the 50-percent-plus-one-vote majority needed to win the race outright on Election Day.

I took on a senior adviser role rather than day-to-day on the campaign, so that I could help Amir and Howard while engaging with my other clients. Callie and Brian, essential members of my Five Points team, worked daily to execute the direct voter contact plan that we'd designed for Amir.

Amir is a big thinker with a vision to enhance Atlanta as a global city, but he never loses sight of the basics needed in any truly livable city. With this in mind, we created a voter engagement initiative for the campaign called "Let's Fix It Together": district residents could let Amir know about infrastructure that needed to be addressed in their neighborhood, whether it was a broken sidewalk, a pothole, or poor signage.

My main role in the campaign's final weeks was to be a constant annoyance to Amir by consistently reiterating that there was no upside to his responding to negative comments allegedly being spread by opponents.

Now, on Election Day, my plan was to drive from precinct to precinct checking turnout numbers, in order to identify where calls needed to be made to registered voters who hadn't yet shown up at the polls during the second half of the day. But my normally trusty gray Honda Accord had broken down at Buddy's gas station, across the street from Manuel's Tavern. So instead of driving around the district to gather data for effective phonebanking throughout the day, I set up shop in the front booth at Manuel's, eating lemon pepper wings, making phone calls, and doing my best to quell my Election Day anxiety.

As on so many past election nights, my role was to focus on the numbers by managing the gathering of final totals from precincts—where they are typically printed and posted within an hour of the polls closing—along with any numbers trickling in through Fulton County's election results website.

As vote totals began to roll in, things were looking good for Amir.

It seemed certain that if there were a runoff, he would be in it—but he also appeared to have a solid chance to win outright before the night was over. Callie and I sat in his upstairs office tracking everything in Excel, letting the beautiful math unfold in front of our eyes. Amir popped in every 15 minutes or so to check, and we continued to add in increasingly Amir-heavy precinct totals received via update calls from Brian, top volunteer Raluca, and our other number-gatherers in the field. Shortly after 10 p.m., we were confident Amir had won outright, avoiding a runoff. The final numbers confirmed this: Amir had earned 55.3 percent of the final vote, securing his spot on the Atlanta City Council.

For me, the rest of that night was awash in Four Roses bourbon, in a celebration that started at Amir's house and ended at Atkins Park on Highland Avenue, a few blocks from Amir's 2009 campaign office.

I'd wanted to work for Amir from the moment I met him. In my view, he was the ideal candidate: someone who wanted to be in elected office to truly serve the community, and was willing and capable of doing all the things needed to win: raising money, hiring the right people, trusting those people, and personally pounding the pavement to meet and engage voters.

Candidates like Amir are rare, and I was honored to be a member of his team.

Since his election, he's proven to be an even better elected official than he is a candidate—which is saying a lot, since he's one of the very best candidates for whom I've worked.

I couldn't have felt more professionally fulfilled as Howard, Amir, Callie, Raluca, and I celebrated into the next morning as we closed down Atkins Park.

But in three short weeks, that happiness would be a distant memory, as my life would come crashing down around me—in part because of those brown-liquor drinks that I loved so much and couldn't stop drinking once I'd started.

September 11, 2010

I T WAS MY first day off since the beginning of April. As I drank my oversized plastic cupful of Jack Daniels swirled together with Coca-Cola while we tailgated before the USC–Georgia football game in Columbia, I still couldn't escape the anxiety and reality of Elena's campaign.

Then my cellphone rang.

It was Elena. I wasn't expecting her to tell me that her opponent had already sent a mailer, and it was showing up paired with a nasty robocall.

First off, I was thinking it was way too early for campaign mail to start because messaging is about repetition and consistency, so mail shouldn't typically start hitting mailboxes until the campaign is ready and able to pay to keep it going through the weekend before Election Day. This was our campaign plan, and, thanks to Elena's stellar fundraising, our first of 19 pieces of direct mail was targeted to land in mailboxes the last week of September; the final piece was to land on October 30, the Saturday before Election Day, November 2.

And I definitely wasn't prepared for the egregious lie that the mailer was spreading. Elena said that it looked like the cover of a copy of the Weekly World News you'd find while waiting in the grocery store checkout line.

The mailer and call that began showing up on Friday alleged that Elena had "stolen" money from DeKalb County school children.

The baseless argument posited that, because Elena's old law firm had represented DeKalb Schools and Elena accepted personal donations from her former colleagues at the firm, the money was somehow taken from kids.

The mailer even had two teen boys holding a photoshopped sign that said: "Hey Elena, please return our school money."

We expected something of this sort from Elena's opponent, because she had run a similar playbook against the previous three Democrats who had run against her and lost.

In fact, Elena had decided to run for the seat in part because she was so disgusted by the negative mail she'd received from her now-opponent against the Democrat challenging her in 2008.

We'd done our homework and had felt prepared for Elena's opponent to replicate what had been successful in the past: negativity, distortion of facts, and touting of her incumbency.

We also prepared to publicly ignore her lies.

My immediate advice to Elena was to try not to internalize it, and to *definitely* not do or say anything in response. The thing about negative campaign messages is a) you don't know who has been exposed to the message and b) you don't know how much money—if any—is being put behind that messaging. In a State House race like Elena's, responding is almost always the wrong move, because you're more likely to spread the negative message to people that hadn't heard it. Then you're playing defense instead of staying on offense to execute your own plan.

For now, nothing needed to be done. We both needed to take a deep breath. She needed to start her door knocking schedule for the day, where we would get a sense of what voters were saying, if anything, about the mail. And I needed to keep drinking with my friend Eric, a Georgia alum who had made the trip from Atlanta to watch his Bulldogs do what they typically did, which was beat the Gamecocks.

But news of the crazy anti-Elena mailer wasn't the only surprise that Saturday in Columbia.

The Georgia defense was no match for our star freshman running back Marcus Lattimore, who was unstoppable, rushing for 182 yards and two touchdowns to lead the Gamecocks to a 17–6 victory. His breakout game was a signal that with this kid in our backfield, the start of something special was unfolding in front of our eyes.

To Eric's credit, he was a great sport about the loss, and I did my best to not gloat too much because as a Gamecocks fan, I knew that over time, Georgia would beat us far more often than we'd beat them.

It was a needed break and a fun weekend.

Upon my return to Atlanta, our team devised a plan to take advantage of the timing of the false mail piece against Elena. The claim from the mailer was so outrageous that an independent fact check could be very helpful to us. *The Atlanta Journal-Constitution* happened to be using the nonpartisan PolitiFact organization to test the veracity of campaign claims. Through back channels, we informed the paper of the mailer and its assertions. They investigated, and ultimately—and very publicly—assigned the nasty claim their worst rating of "Pants on Fire."

"Saying campaign contributions to (Elena) came from money intended for schoolchildren tests the bounds of logic," PolitiFact wrote in their assessment. "Using (this) reasoning, if a lawyer (from Elena's law firm) bought a candy bar at a Wal-Mart, you could accuse the retailer of taking money intended for schoolchildren."

Because the mailer had come out so early in September, we were able to incorporate the "Pants on Fire" rating from PolitiFact into the yet-to-be-designed second half of our mail program, to let voters know about the lies in context. At a time when truth still mattered at least a little bit in politics, the misleading claims had officially been ruled lies by the paper of record. And Elena didn't respond to the claim herself, which could have magnified it more than it had to be before it was dismissed as false by the most trusted news source in Georgia at the time.

Our campaign continued to churn out mail and phone calls to voters, Elena continued to talk to her neighbors at their doors, and the Gamecocks continued to win football games, losing only to future Heisman Trophy Winner Cam Newton and his Auburn Tigers, who would go on to win the National Championship that season.

It was an unforgettable fall where winning was in the air as we headed toward Election Day on November 2.

August 5, 2018

I'D WANTED TO hear the words and music of *Hamilton* for the first time in person—whenever I could finally make it to the Richard Rogers Theater on West 46th Street, a half a block off Times Square—rather than by listening digitally in Atlanta.

It had seemed like half the world had been raving about it since the show and its soundtrack had exploded into the public consciousness in 2015, and remission from tongue cancer seemed a good enough excuse to treat myself to a trip to New York City to finally see the buzzed-about show.

On April 6, Emory University surgeons had excised the cancerous cells from the right side of my tongue and made a six-inch incision in my neck in order to remove lymph nodes, which were then examined to learn whether the cancer was limited to my tongue or had spread.

The news had been good: my squamous cell carcinoma hadn't spread, and, after successful surgery, there was no cancer in my body. Because nerves in my neck had to be cut, I had earned an overnight hospital stay and a month of recovery. I'd been left without sensation in a swath of my skin from the middle of my throat, along the right side of my neck, and over to my shoulder, but I was fortunate to dodge chemo and radiation treatment.

I took my seat. Before I knew it, the three Schuyler sisters were singing from the stage as if directly to me, reminding me how lucky I was to be alive, and that I was in the greatest city in the world.

This was my 11th trip to New York since March 2014. This was where I felt more at peace than anywhere else, and I'd designed my visit to include every necessary component for my perfect remission celebration weekend in Manhattan.

I was staying in a tiny one-bedroom apartment on Avenue A at 14th Street in the East Village, the setting for *Rent* and my favorite New York neighborhood. Thanks to Airbnb, I could get a brief glimpse of what it was like to actually live in the city, rather than get the typical tourist experience of sterile, characterless comfort provided by a big-name hotel.

I had plans to take in my favorite comedic storyteller Mike Birbiglia's *The New One* at the Cherry Lane Theater in the West Village, catch a flick at the newly-renovated Film Forum—my favorite movie house on earth—and treat myself to a thoughtfully-curated weekend menu.

I'd hit David Chang's Momofuku for a perfect, smoky bowl of ramen, then later, stop by Luzzo's to drizzle Calabrian chile-infused oil over an airy, Napoli-style pizza from their 120-year-old coal oven. I'd swing by Pig & Khao to sit at Leah Cohen's chef's bar and devour a plate of grilled pork jowl with acidic, charred Brussels, settle in for a late-night seating to take on Eric Ripert's tasting menu at Le Bernardin, and follow-up *Hamilton* with an early dinner at Tom Colicchio's Craft.

And finally, the Braves were fortuitously in town, so my friends Joshua and Leslie, who had each worked on campaigns with me when they lived in Atlanta, came from Brooklyn to join me at Citi Field to watch Atlanta beat eventual 2018 Cy Young Award winner Jacob deGrom and the Mets in a 2–1 pitcher's duel on Friday, the eight-month anniversary of my sobriety.

Earlier that afternoon, I had visited the Alcoholics Anonymous World Services offices near Columbia University on Riverside Drive to browse the AA archive. It's basically a mini museum, with original books and writing by founders Bill W. and Dr. Bob.

The most striking items in the archive were the plaque and logbook from The Ground Zero Group, which met across the street from the World Trade Center site; members took six-hour shifts to enable anyone needing an AA meeting during the site clean-up between September 29 and November 30, 2001, to find fellowship. The plaque was made of steel from the fallen towers, and the logbook was filled with thoughts and prayers from the group. I couldn't conceive of how difficult sobriety must have been for them and so many others in 2001. This exhibit gave me new perspective on my sobriety and my post-9/11 anxiety issues.

Afterwards, I'd taken the Number 1 Train several stops south to Barney Greengrass, an Upper Westside favorite of Anthony Bourdain, who had died by suicide just two months earlier, on June 8. As an ode to my favorite food storyteller, I was there to eat his go-to breakfast—Nova Scotia Lox and egg scramble and a bagel.

As I ate this salty, creamy plate of goodness and washed it down with the syrupy-sweet Dr. Brown's Black Cherry soda that Dad had introduced me to as a kid, I was reminded that my tongue no longer hurt.

My tongue had begun hurting midway through 2017. I'd been in constant pain but had been too consumed with juggling my consulting work with candidates and fundraising work with nonprofits to go to the doctor. If my tongue hurt too much, I'd numb the physical pain with bourbon, in the same way I'd learned to dispatch my emotional torment.

When I decided to get sober, I'd also finally taken myself to the doctor for a look at my tongue.

My primary care doc hadn't been concerned but also wasn't

sure, so he'd sent me to an ear, nose, and throat specialist. That doctor hadn't been able to come to a conclusion either, and had encouraged me to see a dentist. When I finally visited my dentist in mid-February 2018, a white spot had developed on my tongue that he wanted to biopsy immediately. We'd agreed to schedule the procedure for Friday, February 23.

My brother Bryan, now 35, would come to Atlanta from Greenville—where he's worked as a literal rocket scientist for General Electric since 2006—to pick me up after the procedure and take care of me, because they'd be putting me under anesthesia. This was the first time we'd be together on February 23 and 24 since Dad died in 1996.

Having my tongue cut open and stitched back up isn't the most fun I've ever had, so the next few days had been centered around a liquidish-based diet of chocolate pudding, Mott's applesauce, and strawberry Jell-O.

For the first time in my life, I'd been feeling optimistic. There was no way I had cancer—other than a lone cigarette on the bus in eighth grade, I'd never used tobacco, and there was no history of cancer in my blood-related family.

But, late on Tuesday afternoon February 27, I'd received the terrifying news that it *was* cancer.

My dentist had ordered a CT scan of my head and neck and a consult with his recommended Emory University surgeon. Four days later, on March 3, I would be 90 days sober, and after the call from my dentist, I knew the obsession to drink had been excised from my mind: instead of heading to a bar to drink away this terrifying news, I'd gone directly from my office to a 5:45 p.m. AA meeting, shared about my cancer diagnosis, and then had dinner with a sober friend, Sam, who was also a doctor and did his best to calm my nerves.

The weeks after my April 6 surgery had been spent drinking fruit-based smoothies and homemade soups brought by sweet friends who'd visited as I recovered, providing physical and emotional sustenance. And now, in addition to being in remission, I'd lived through five more months of successful sobriety as I took in Lin-Manuel Miranda's masterpiece, which brought together my love for innovative storytelling, social justice, history, politics, writing, musical theater, and New York City itself.

On this Sunday, I was living and thriving—as I typically was when I was visiting New York. There, even when I was alone, I never felt isolated. But I'd never been able to bring the version of me that exists there back with me to Atlanta.

Once I returned home from this pitch-perfect weekend—even as grateful as I was to be in remission—my mind was still trying to trick me into believing I didn't deserve to live.

December 25, 2003

I'D NEVER HAD a lonelier Christmas.

I was fighting my depression as I scavenged for dinner at an Elkhart, Indiana, gas station, almost 750 miles away from Bee and Papa's house in Blythewood.

I'd awakened that morning to our annual routine of lining up in reverse age order—Abby, then Bryan, then Gina, then me—to then discover our gifts from "Santa" in our designated spots around the living room.

We'd spent Christmas morning together in this same place since 1981, when Bee and Papa moved back to Papa's family homestead in rural Richland County. Our family had lots of rituals, but Christmas Eve and Christmas Day were the most important of them all to me. After church on Christmas Eve, we'd head to "the country" to settle in for crispy chicken wings and salty raw fries from Wings & Ale, and then dessert—usually Mom's M&M cookies and Villa Tronco cheesecake.

Then, Pam and Mom would embrace their role as elves, passing out presents from the family. We would read *The Night Before Christmas* out loud before we opened our family presents. The kids would then play Rummy or Phase 10 while watching *National Lampoon's Christmas Vacation*.

And finally, we'd head to bed, so "Santa" could have full reign of the house when he arrived to place our gifts in each one of our spots in the living room.

Even as adults, we'd wake up to Mom and Pam telling us to line up to take our annual picture before being ushered into the living room to discover what delightful gifts Santa had left for each of us. In between our digging through presents, emptying out our stockings, and going back to sleep, Papa and Bee would serve us pillowy Buttermilk Angel biscuits brushed with melted butter, salty country ham, and fresh-squeezed orange juice, which was typically Gina's job to make.

On this Christmas I'd rushed through our morning routine because I had to head to the airport, fly back to South Bend alone, and then drive to work in Elkhart. At 25 years old, this would be my first Christmas night alone.

Audrey and I had moved to Indiana in July for her to start law school at Notre Dame, and I was still working for *The Elkhart Truth* for a few more weeks before I'd join the *South Bend Tribune*'s Michigan bureau. I had the least seniority at the paper, so I was stuck working on Christmas even though Audrey had several weeks off for her winter break.

I was spending this Christmas Thursday listening to a police scanner, in case anything happened that was worth covering. Nothing worth writing about occurred, and on Friday, after another day of doing very little, I flew right back to Columbia for the rest of our Christmas break.

That night was the loneliest, most depressing Christmas I'd ever experienced.

No family. No Audrey. No Sandberg. No dinner.

But I was able to trick my mind by reflecting on far more memorable Christmas experiences.

I remembered 1994, when Christmas fell on a Sunday, so Papa prepared a full Christmas morning service for our family, and my girlfriend Sara joined us to hear our favorite retired Southern Baptist preacher do what he had done best for decades, before his retirement the year before.

I remembered Christmas Eve 1987, peering with Gina through the slats in the door between the den and the back bedrooms, after we'd heard more laughter from the adults than ever before. Luckily, Wally was videotaping everything with his new JVC video camera, so we were ultimately able to see the whole scene of Santa actually showing up. I can still see Dad laughing on that tape.

In the journal Bee gave me in 2002, she wrote of the most "hilarious laughter ever" by my dad that night. "The front doorbell rang," Bee wrote, noting that everyone inside the house knew the gate to the driveway was closed at night. "Wally went to the front door and hollered, 'Who is it?' A voice came back: 'Who the h*ll do you think it is?'"

Then Wally invited in a "big, fat, round" Santa Claus, who came in "joking and carrying on." Each of the adults then received a present from Santa. Bee and Papa had given them earlier to Papa's cousin, Frank, who had dressed up to surprise the adults after the kids all went to bed. "It was a hoot," Bee remembered. "Steve could not contain himself."

I also remembered Christmas 1986, when my dad was far less happy, and broke the news to me that Santa wasn't real. We were sitting at the airport waiting for our flight to visit Dad's parents, his younger sister and brother, Joan and Wayne, and their families in Colorado. I was eight, and now would have to keep this secret from Gina, Bryan, and Abby for years. He and Mom were separated, so breaking that news to me must have been a unilateral parenting choice.

My second Christmas was spent in Illinois with the Romig side of the family. Mom wasn't happy being away from her family in 1979. "The whole time we were there we couldn't really go anywhere because there was so much snow," she told me. But I was learning things and connecting with cartoons. "Ruth taught you to go down the stairs from the bedrooms by sitting down on them and bumping down," Sandra remembered about my paternal grandmother. "Oh, and you thought Charlie Brown was the best!"

I remembered Christmas 1995, the final Christmas with all 10 of us. Gina and I had decided to spend the night with Bee and Papa on "Christmas Eve-Eve" to help get everything ready, because Papa was very sick and Bee needed our help.

It was a terrifying night, trying to sleep on the pullout couch in the living room while hearing Papa coughing in a way that seemed like every whoop could be his final breath.

I approached our family traditions that year with the idea that this could be our final Christmas together, so I decided to soak it all in. Sadly, I was right; it just never crossed my mind that my dad would be the person missing in 1996. That was the first Christmas since 1979 that we had lost a close family member since the previous Christmas.

Mom tells me that my first Christmas, in 1978, was spent with Bee's extended family at the home of her parents, Mem and Pap, as Mom called her grandparents. "I remember Pap holding you and playing with you," she said of my great-grandfather. "He was not well that day, and sadly, he died less than two weeks later."

But in Christmas 1980, we had a new arrival, as Gina had joined our family less than three months earlier. Later, Pam and Mom had the adorable idea of dressing Gina and me in matching Christmas pajamas; that remained a tradition for years, ultimately including Bryan in 1982 and Abby in 1984. One of my favorite pictures is of Gina and me sometime in the mid-1980s, sitting on Bee and Papa's black-and-white striped couch in matching red-and-white Christmas pajamas for our annual reading of *The Night Before Christmas*.

I was fortunate to be able to tap into all of these wonderful family Christmas memories to help me overcome my loneliness and depression on this dark Christmas in the middle of rural Indiana.

July 27, 2014

COOPERSTOWN IS A village in the middle of New York state that's home to fewer than 2,000 people on most days. But during one glorious weekend each summer, it's transformed—when around 300,000 baseball fans descend upon the historic hamlet for the annual Hall of Fame induction ceremony hosted by the National Baseball Hall of Fame and Museum.

After a Major League Baseball player retires, he must wait at least six years before being eligible for induction. So, when Greg Maddux and Tom Glavine retired after the 2008 seasons, I circled July 2014 on my mental calendar.

I'd watched Maddux and Glavine lead the Braves pitching staff, along with John Smoltz, from 1993 through 2002, and if those two were going to be inducted together into the Hall of Fame, I wanted to be there. As a bonus, Bobby Cox, who managed those great Braves teams of the 1990s that I watched growing up, was also being inducted. There was no way I'd miss out on this monumental day in Braves history. So Audrey and I flew into Albany, rented a car, and drove the 70 miles west.

Joshua had driven up from New York City to join us for the trip through the museum, lunch, and the induction ceremony. After today's induction, Audrey and I would turn in our car and ride back to the city with him so we could extend our trip to my favorite vacation spot.

This Sunday afternoon was going to be filled with speeches from Maddux, Glavine, and Cox, along with three other inductees: White Sox slugger Frank Thomas, Yankees manager Joe Torre, and Tony LaRussa—who had managed the A's, Cardinals, and White Sox, but whom we especially loved for founding the Animal Rescue Foundation (ARF).

Our morning would be spent reveling in the museum itself. We saw Glavine's Cy Young Award from 1991 and the ball and uniform from his 300th victory, which he unfortunately earned in 2007 playing with our rival New York Mets before he returned to the Braves for his final season in 2008.

We saw the American Tobacco Company baseball cards of Joe Tinker, Johnny Evers, and Frank Chance, the Cubs infield trio made famous in the 1910 poem "Baseball's Sad Lexicon," in which Franklin Pierce Adams detailed the pain of a New York Giants fan watching these three men complete double play after double play to foil his team's offense.

> These are the saddest of possible words:
> Tinker to Evers to Chance.
> Trio of Bear-cubs, fleeter than birds,
> Tinker to Evers to Chance.
> Ruthlessly pricking our gonfalon bubble,
> Making a Giant hit into a double --
> Words that are weighty with nothing but trouble:
> Tinker to Evers to Chance.

The legends of the game came to life around us throughout our self-guided tour as we laid eyes on Mickey Mantle's jersey, Ty Cobb's glove, Willie Mays's 535th home run ball, Ryne Sandberg's 1984 MVP bat, Joe DiMaggio's spikes, and Kerry Wood's cap from his 20-strikeout game. We also saw props from baseball movie history: Robert Redford's "Wonderboy" bat from *The Natural,* Geena Davis's Rockford Peaches uniform from *A League of Their Own,* and Kevin Costner's Durham Bulls jersey from *Bull Durham.*

We spent a whole hour in the Plaque Gallery, taking pictures with the induction plaques of Ryne Dee Sandberg and Jack Roosevelt Robinson (the namesakes of our Hall of Fame yellow labs) and reading (and taking pictures of) at least 100 of the more than 300 Hall of Famers' plaques, which detailed their greatness and contributions to the game I'd loved ever since the mid-1980s, when Bee had bought me my first pack of Topps baseball cards and taught me how to score a game.

When Maddux and Glavine retired after the 2008 season, Bee and I were still talking baseball all the time, and we'd imagined watching their eventual induction together.

As Audrey, Joshua, and I navigated every inch of the three floors of history, memories, and artifacts, I couldn't stop thinking about Bee and Papa, and how they never had the opportunity to experience this revered place before they died. In the years before she died in August 2012, Alzheimer's had slowly stolen Bee's mind from her, and from us. Our weekly phone calls ultimately disintegrated to her barely recognizing me when we were together. Then, just two weeks before this trip, Papa joined Bee, succumbing at 92 to the heart problems that had ailed him since I was in elementary school.

Today would be one of the banner days in my life as a baseball fan, but I wished with all my heart I could share it with Bee and Papa.

September 30, 2012

AUDREY SAT ON our hardwood floor with the wiggly puppy in her lap as I brought Sandberg over to meet his new little brother. Robinson had just come home to us from Charleston, where he'd been born on August 13; we'd first met him there a week earlier.

Our boys were both yellow Labrador retrievers, and both named after Hall of Fame second basemen—my Cubs hero Ryne Sandberg, and Jackie Robinson, a hero of the world as the first Black player to play in a Major League Baseball game on April 15, 1947.

As a puppy, Robinson was the lightest shade of yellow and the best kind of trouble, from the moment we picked him out from the litter. His biological dad belonged to one of Audrey's best friends.

At nine years old, Sandberg was darker, but still light brown. He'd slowly learned to live without sight after being diagnosed with progressive retinal atrophy in July 2005, when he was only two-and-a-half years old.

Sandberg was one of the sweetest, most resilient dogs ever; he'd taught himself to run in tight circles in our fenced-in backyard so he could run fast without crashing into anything. But he wasn't prepared for whatever this thing was that kept trying to jump on his face and scamper underneath his belly while he was standing. Robinson loved his big brother, but it took six months for Sandberg to reciprocate consistently.

In March 2003, during our first year of marriage, we'd decided that it was time to get a puppy, so we'd looked in the *Herald-Journal*'s classified ads for Labrador retriever puppies. Audrey had grown up with labs and knew how to train them. Bryan and I had never had pets growing up, so I didn't know what to expect from a puppy as we drove to Boiling Springs, North Carolina, to meet Sandberg, whom we'd already named.

When we walked into the pen where Sandberg and his siblings were running around, Audrey had taken the time to meet several of his brothers and sisters. But I saw him and scooped him up immediately, while Audrey tried to calm down his crazy brother, who was white with blue eyes and gnawing sweetly but ferociously on her pant leg.

After spending time with our new puppy outside of the pen, we'd agreed that he was our guy.

Audrey trained Robinson just as masterfully as she had Sandberg, who definitely was smarter and caught on faster than his new little brother.

On March 20, 2013, we celebrated Sandberg's 10th birthday. By that time, Robinson was a gangly, skinny guy who was now far too big to run underneath his big brother. This was likely the key reason for their newfound friendship. Sadly, their time together would be short-lived.

Just six weeks later, on Sunday, May 5, we had to say goodbye to our sweet Sandberg after he came down with acute pancreatitis. Most dogs can recover from this affliction, but Sandberg was so tough that it wasn't until he stopped eating the Thursday before that there was any indication that something was wrong. By the time they did surgery on Saturday to figure out what was happening, it was too late.

I will always be grateful that we were given the opportunity to sit with Sandberg and hold him as he left us, and equally thankful that Robinson was there to greet us when we returned to the house after that terrible morning, when our hearts were split wide open as we lost our first furbaby.

Robinson is now eight and has had his own health issues—including cancer, for which he's in remission, like his human dad. Since 2015 he's been a time-share dog, living half the time with me and half with Audrey following our divorce. Like Sandberg before him, Robinson brings so much joy and unconditional love into my life. When I'm anxious or depressed, he is there to take me on walks, give me kisses, and climb into my lap as if he were still a pocket-sized puppy.

I could not have dreamed of two sweeter boys to make me a doggy dad and teach me so many new dimensions to loving another living thing.

June 22, 2002

BEING MARRIED IN the church I grew up attending wasn't our first choice. But the location of our wedding was never as important as was the man we wanted to marry us. He just happened to be a Southern Baptist preacher.

The Catholic church wouldn't allow a non-Catholic pastor to perform a marriage ceremony inside one of their places of worship, so Audrey's church wasn't an option. The simplest alternative was to be married at North Trenholm Baptist Church in Columbia, which had played host to my Baptism and my dad's memorial service. That way, Papa could preside over our wedding as we said our vows in front of hundreds of guests and our extra-large wedding party of nine bridesmaids and groomsmen.

Audrey and I had begun our wedding march on April 28, 2001. I believed I'd convinced her that I was planning to propose during our scheduled trip to New York in June with Mom and Bryan, which allowed me to devise a sneaky proposal at the end of April.

I'd always been a romantic, and I believed in this idea of "the one." Audrey was intelligent, hilarious, kind, beautiful, and seemingly perfect for me.

As I sat in that booth at Villa Tronco with a plate of rich, melted-mozzarella-and-red-sauce-covered veal parmesan in front of me,

I was so nervous I couldn't eat a bite. Our evening was to start in that booth, and then move a half-mile away to the back steps of the South Carolina State Capitol, where I would actually propose. Then we'd meet our families for dessert to celebrate our engagement.

The proposal went as planned. We were happily engaged, and I was really hungry. The diamond in the platinum band on Audrey's left ring finger came from the engagement ring my dad had given my mom when he asked her to spend the rest of their lives together.

In the time between that Saturday and this one 14 months later, our world had changed dramatically following the September 11 attacks and my dual diagnosis of generalized anxiety disorder and clinical depression. Thanks to my daily meds, I was beginning to experience my life with more stability.

But as I sat in the groom's room with our groomsmen, I was even more nervous than I had been sitting in that booth at Villa Tronco with Audrey on the day I proposed.

Luckily, the universe gave me a small distraction to draw my mind away from the monumental nature of this day, and the deeply felt absence of the man who should have been there to stand beside me: baseball made its way into my wedding day to reduce my stress. Our Gamecocks had made it to the final game of the College World Series in Omaha, where they were at that moment taking on the Texas Longhorns. (They would lose, but that was typical Gamecocks.)

The weekend before, my bachelor weekend in Atlanta had, unsurprisingly, revolved around Braves baseball.

Most bachelor parties in Atlanta feature one or more strip clubs, but mine didn't include any. I'd opted instead to take the guys in our wedding party to watch the pitches of Greg Maddux and Tom Glavine dance around the bats of the Boston Red Sox. As a bonus, John Smoltz had closed out Maddux's win on Saturday. Glavine had lost on Sunday, but watching three future Hall of Famers in two days was absolutely my ideal bachelor party.

But for the always-stark absence of my dad, everything else about our wedding day seemed perfect. We had planned our ideal ceremony with Papa at the helm, and all of our friends and family were joining us for the ceremony and then the reception at the Columbia Museum of Art.

As Papa married us that afternoon, I truly believed Audrey was the one, and that we would spend our lives together.

November 23, 1984

I T WAS FRIDAY. Yesterday, on Thanksgiving, we'd filled our bellies with turkey, green beans, brown rice (the unhealthy kind made with French onion soup, beef consommé, and lots of butter), and my great Aunt Tootsie's famous Red Velvet Cake.

We'd watched two exciting Thanksgiving Day NFL games—the Cowboys had held on to beat the Patriots 20–17, and the Lions had upset the Packers, 31–28—and I'd hung out across the street from Tootsie's house with Carolyn, who was six like me, and her older sister Sandy, who was eight.

Sandy, Carolyn, and I always had fun together once a year, when my family visited the West Ashley section of Charleston for Thanksgiving at Bee's sister's house. We'd talk for hours on the dock behind their house on the Stono River. We'd act out *Grease* as we watched it over and over on VHS. We'd try to shoot pool on the red felt table in their playroom. And we'd sneak into their wood-paneled hot tub on their back porch.

Before we could do anything this afternoon, at 1 p.m. we had to watch *Days of our Lives*, which Papa, Tootsie, and Mom also watched, and which became a staple of our holidays. That particular episode is the first one I really remember; it was a literal cliffhanger as Roman Brady fought his nemesis Stefano DiMera on the top of a cliff before being shot and falling to his "death."

After *Days* was over, most of the adults wanted to watch the conclusion of the only college football game that day, in which Boston College ultimately beat Miami, 47–45 on a last-second Hail Mary touchdown pass by some kid named Doug Flutie. I don't remember the end of the game personally, but I do remember that the promised fried shrimp dinner was delayed so that they didn't have to miss the end.

On Monday, I was back at school at North Springs Elementary, so it would be a long time before I actually saw how the cliffhanger on *Days* played out—on a VHS tape, sometime in the mid-1990s. Because *Days* was a show I watched with Papa and my mom during holidays and summer vacation, that made it special. (*Days* would become a bigger part of my life in middle school, when I began taping and watching it every day when I got home. I would choose to immerse myself in the stories and drama of Salem rather than create my own stories in the real world, as my anxiety led me to isolate more and more into the safety of movies, television, books, and sports.)

Two years after that Thanksgiving, during third grade, I would be introduced to the book that led me to embrace reading—and ultimately writing—in a consistent, passionate way.

Susan Hinton became a household name in 1967 with the publishing of what's considered the first YA novel, *The Outsiders*. Under the name S. E. Hinton, she wrote about the kids in the two rival gangs at her high school in Tulsa, Oklahoma, from the male perspective, but through the mind of the insightful 16-year-old female writer she was.

The sensitive sides of Ponyboy Curtis and Johnny Cade would be deeply formative models for me, as would the introduction of the Robert Frost poem they loved, "Nothing Gold Can Stay":

Nature's first green is gold,
Her hardest hue to hold.
Her early leaf's a flower;
But only so an hour.
Then leaf subsides to leaf.
So Eden sank to grief,
So dawn goes down to day.
Nothing gold can stay.

S. E. Hinton would show me that—even in the midst of the haves-versus-have-nots gang violence between the Greasers and the Socs (short for Socials) that centers the story—it was acceptable for boys to love poetry and watch sunsets.

We would live with Bee and Papa during third grade after my parents separated—a confusing time from which I have few memories—and I would find solace in reading books like *The Outsiders*, watching *Days* with Papa, and listening to the Braves with Bee. As my grandparents and their home provided stability, these fictional characters and stories would give me an escape during this perplexing and scary time.

Before I knew it, by fourth grade, my parents would be back together. We'd all be living together again, in a new house in a new neighborhood closer to my school, where Mom taught second grade. I'd have my own room again to hide in, losing myself in books and movies and television to escape the uncertainty I felt about the stability of my family.

July 29, 1993

TODAY WAS A day of firsts.

I went to Wyoming. I watched a rodeo. I ate bison. I saw John Elway throw a football in front of me.

This memorable day began at my aunt and uncle's house outside of Boulder, Colorado; then took us an hour northwest to Greeley for Broncos training camp at the University of Northern Colorado, then another hour north to Cheyenne Frontier Days, held the last full week of each July.

Almost a week earlier, Dad had taken me, Bryan, and Mom on vacation for a week in Colorado, where we stayed with his sister, Joan, her husband, Ron, and our cousins, Annaliese and Eric. It had been such an eventful trip.

We'd been to three baseball games at Mile High Stadium, where the Colorado Rockies were playing their inaugural season. We'd gone to a gold mine in Idaho Springs and learned how they originally panned for gold. And we'd gone to the top of Mount Evans on the highest paved road in North America, which sits at 14,271 feet above sea level in the Rocky Mountains.

The beauty of the places we saw was unparalleled in my life to this point. And now we were winding down the trip in the Native American Village section of Cheyenne Frontier Days.

I was looking for a souvenir to take back to Columbia, and that's when it jumped out at me. Hand-written in black calligraphy on a piece of light brown parchment was a beautiful poem that I wouldn't have to memorize, because I could take it with me.

It was said to be a Native American poem, but years later I learned differently—a fact that doesn't detract from its power. On this piece of paper, it was titled "I'm Not Here."

Don't stand at my grave and weep
For I'm not there. I do not sleep.
I am a thousand winds that blow.
I am the diamond glints on snow.
I am the sunlight on ripened grain.
I am the gentle autumn's rain.
When you awaken in morning's hush
I am the swift uplifting rush
Of quiet birds in circle flight.
I am the soft stars that shine at night.
Do not stand at my grave and cry
I am not there. I did not die

I loved these words the moment I read them, but it would be much later when I'd begin to understand what they would mean in my life.

Dad left us on February 24, 1996, and we buried him at Crescent Hill Memorial Gardens on Two Notch Road in Columbia. He's not there, but he continues to live on inside my mind through the legacy of his words and actions—good and bad.

April 5, 1995

THE FIRST WEEK of April was my favorite sports week of the year. It began with the Final Four and ended with the Masters in Augusta, with the best day of every year—Opening Day in Major League Baseball—falling in between.

Even though there was no baseball that week in 1995, the baseball strike that began the previous August (and led to the first-ever World Series cancellation) had finally come to an end on Monday, April 3, the day before the season was supposed to begin with non-union replacement players.

That Monday night, the 31–1 UCLA Bruins beat the 32–6 Arkansas Razorbacks 89–78 for the NCAA basketball title. Now, on this Wednesday, I was missing school for my first trip to Augusta National as part of my unpaid internship for the sports department at WOLO, Columbia's ABC affiliate.

My sports journalism career had begun at WOLO, as I learned to edit sports highlights for the 11 p.m. newscast. Now, just a few weeks after my first night, I'd be making my sports journalism debut in my birthplace of Augusta—on the same day that a kid from Stanford named Tiger Woods was making his Masters debut as the US Amateur Champion.

Woods's five-over-par finish landed him in 41st place, while I expertly lugged the camera bag for WOLO's on-air sports team, Terry and Cory, from hole to hole during the tournament's practice round.

I also proved to be quite proficient at making Augusta National's signature egg salad and pimento cheese sandwiches disappear.

The only reason I had the time for this internship was that I had decided a few months earlier not to go out for Varsity baseball so that I could "focus on journalism" at our school paper, *The Viking Shield*.

Even though my journalism experiences in the spring of 1995 began to lay the foundation for what would ultimately be my career, that wasn't the real reason I didn't try out for baseball. I'd played Junior Varsity baseball during my freshman and sophomore years at Spring Valley. But junior year, in what was a key example of how my anxiety hijacked my decision making, I was so scared of failing that I took control by choosing not to try out at all. Instead of facing and overcoming that fear, I traded my love of playing baseball for journalism, a place where I was becoming fearless.

I wish I'd been able to be as fearless on the baseball field as most of my teammates seemed to be, but despite having some talent as a hitter and in the field at second base, I gave it up for fear of not being good enough.

If only I'd remembered the insight of Frank Herbert's "Litany Against Fear" from *Dune*, to shift my perspective:

> I must not fear. Fear is the mind-killer. Fear is the little death
> that brings total obliteration. I will face my fear. I will permit
> it to pass over me and through me. And when it has gone
> past, I will turn the inner eye to see its path. Where the fear
> has gone there will be nothing. Only I will remain.

As a 17-year-old in 1995, the world was changing fast. In a short period, I watched the domestic terror of the Oklahoma City Bombing in April; ended my relationship with Sara, not long after the anniversary of our July 1994 wreck; participated in the launch of Windows 95 and America Online in August; and joined the world in being riveted by the O. J. Simpson trial.

Starting with my WOLO internship and continuing into the summer of 1995—when I had my first taste of covering Capital City Bombers baseball through taking over as managing editor of *The Viking Shield* at the beginning of my senior year—I was finding my way into the two things that would define my life for the next decade: journalism and anxiety.

The pen, the keyboard, and the newsroom were the only places I felt any confidence at all, so I put my energy into writing as often as possible, disconnecting myself from places I felt uncomfortable, which was everywhere else.

My other safe space was my room: reading, watching baseball, *Days* or movies, listening to music (U2, Rage Against the Machine, Pearl Jam, Counting Crows), and recreating every player and their stats from the 1984 baseball season, when Ryne Sandberg won the MVP, so that I could use them to play my Tony LaRussa Baseball PC video game.

While I was hiding from the world, my nuclear family was entering its final months.

On October 28, 1995, Dad and I would watch and celebrate as the Braves won their first World Series with a 1–0 Game Six victory in Atlanta over the Cleveland Indians. There would be no way I could know that in 120 days, he would be dead.

February 24, 1996

THE THREAD RUNNING through my relationship with my dad during my teen years was anger.

Him with me. Me with him. Us with each other.

But I could've never foreseen the fury I felt in this moment, because what was happening seemed totally unimaginable.

I would never know everything that had led to my dad's decision to end his life hours earlier. Answers would be limited to guesses, assumptions, and the words written in his three letters. I read the letter he wrote to me, but I didn't believe he was dead. I was livid, and in those first few minutes I believed that everything that was happening was an elaborate hoax by a sick man.

I was only right about the sick part. It was clear from his words and final action that my dad's brilliant mind had been broken by fear, pain, and illness.

Once I had composed myself, I called Chris, my high school newspaper's faculty adviser, to tell him that my dad was dead.

Although only 26 years old, Chris did a great job of playing the multiple roles of teacher, mentor, and friend to all of his students who worked on *The Viking Shield*, which was the only place in my life where I truly felt like I belonged on a daily basis.

Chris said he'd be right over, and was the first non-family visitor to arrive at our house to support Mom, Bryan, and me in our earliest hours of this new, Steve-less world.

I was numb, and I didn't know what to say or do, or how so many people knew to come to our house. But I soaked up the endless stream of love from my newspaper friends, our church friends, Mom's teacher friends, and, of course, members of our extended family.

For once, I didn't want to be alone in my room.

In between visits, I kept reading and re-reading the letter he wrote to me, searching for answers that would never arrive, no matter how many times I examined his final words. Those words made it clear that he believed his death was the only way he could support us financially.

Since we'd been in Alabama visiting Tuscaloosa only seven days earlier, it seemed no coincidence to me that the money needed for me to attend the University of Alabama was a factor in his deeply flawed decision. The third sentence of his letter confirmed this: "I want you to go to the college of your choice," he acknowledged.

He also made sure to let me know that the journalism career I'd dreamed of since I was 12 wasn't ideal in his mind. "I am cynical of the press, and extremely disappointed in the quality of most television programming. To your desire to go into journalism, I think a lot of what is on television is a sorry commentary on our social fabric," he wrote, ignoring my desire to write for a newspaper.

His letter laid out the things I "should do" in college, which was essentially a reiteration of the things he believed I hadn't done in high school. "If you will commit to taking on in college all that is required of you, in a serious and conscientious manner, you should do well," he posited. "However, if you work diligently and successfully only on the topics you like, you will have a difficult time."

His goodbye to me, like our relationship, wasn't filled with much love or light—just instructions, establishing a lifelong bar that would never be reachable by me, because now his disappointment in me was frozen in time.

The contrast between the horror of that morning and the outpouring of love that would follow in the coming days was stark. I found myself saying over and over to myself and my visitors that I needed to figure out how to talk about my feelings. After reading his letter, it seemed clear to me that if he'd found a way to talk to other people about the fears he detailed, he might still be alive.

But he was gone, as was the world in which I had lived—shattered into dust and razor-sharp shards to cut me forever, rather than into pieces that could be reassembled.

He seemed to want his letter to point me toward a plan for living by which he himself had experienced success, but it only reinforced in me that I was a disappointment to him. Even in his final moments, I had filled him with frustration over my inability to replicate the work ethic and discipline he'd modeled for me all my life. He seemed to believe that if I followed his instructions, there might be hope for me in this world. But those words now conflicted with his final choice.

Which was I to follow: the example of his discipline, or the example of his death?

January 20, 2012

FOR MANY YEARS, I've had my butt kicked in pool by some of my closest friends. But no one kicked my butt like the man who taught me how to play.

Steve Romig didn't let you win. Whether you were a friend on the tennis court or his older son at the pool table, you had to earn it. Sometimes I did. Mostly, I didn't.

In his suicide letter, he wrote that he wished he had been able to buy us a pool table for our house.

"One thing I am so disappointed in my life was that I always seemed to get into jobs that kept me constantly working and never giving me the ability to spend all the time that I wanted with you," he admitted. "I wanted to have a rec room with a pool table. I wanted to have some ATVs so we could drive through the woods and jet boats to get on the lake. I hope you are willing to get involved with other people who like to do these kinds of things and broaden your horizons, since I wasn't able to expose you to those types of fun things."

Unfortunately, I am my father's son when it comes to working all the time, at the expense of relaxing and enjoying outdoor activities. But my nonstop work in 2010 had led to this particular day in 2012, when one of his dreams for me was coming true.

My pool table was being installed.

One of the best moments of my life had come late on the evening of November 2, 2010, when I gave Elena the news that she had beaten her incumbent Republican opponent and was now state representative-elect.

Then, before we left the Red Clay Democrats' election night party at the Georgia Tech Hotel and Conference Center, I'd been able to write win-bonus checks to Leslie and Carolyn, critical members of our campaign team. My win-bonus check came later, and I would spend it to listen to my dad, for once.

On this Friday morning in 2012, my new pool table was being installed in what had been Audrey's and my dining room. As the work was progressing, I reflected on all the times I had lost to my dad, and the contrast between that and winning on November 2, 2010.

In the terrible political year for Democrats, Elena was one of only 12 Democrats across the country—and the only one in Georgia between 2009 and 2016—to defeat an incumbent Republican at the state legislative level.

After back-to-back campaigns, I'd taken the rest of 2010 off to recharge before joining Elena for the 2011 legislative session as her chief of staff. I learned a lot during my session under Georgia's Gold Dome, but working in the legislature hadn't been for me. I was ready to either get back to nonprofit work or working on political campaigns.

Now, a year later, in 2012, I was excited to have this new toy in my house to distract my mind from my job as political director for a statewide political action committee.

I'd found the perfect combination of nonprofit work and political campaigns, but I'd become burnt out on politics, my nerves were frayed, and my mental health was becoming a daily swirl of nastiness.

I desperately needed a change and a break, because the job I had was only exacerbating my ongoing anxiety. I was finding myself again experiencing panic attacks, paralyzing depression, and vivid thoughts of suicide. So, I decided to quit my job to try to get my mental health under control and determine what I wanted professionally.

On March 19, just days after resigning from my political director job, I was standing 100 feet from President Obama at Tyler Perry Studios in southwest Atlanta as he spoke to a hand-selected crowd of about 500 Atlanta young professionals for the kickoff of Gen44, an effort to engage young professionals in the president's re-election campaign.

As inspiring as it was to hear from the president, I knew as I listened that I'd made the correct choice, and was excited to see where life after political campaigns would take me.

It had been an honor to serve in campaign leadership positions for public-servant leaders like Elena, but I was beginning to believe that I wanted to focus on creating community impact in nonpolitical ways, or at least in nonpartisan ways.

I'd also recently learned that the executive director position at VOX Teen Communications was open.

VOX's visionary founder, Rachel, was stepping back from the role she'd originated in 1993, when she and a group of teens launched VOX: a citywide, nonprofit teen newspaper and after-school program where teens came together from across Atlanta for leadership development, journalism, and self-expression.

Two years earlier, I'd worked on a project with VOX as part of a year-long leadership class. I loved the organization and knew that this could be the perfect fit for my skill set and passion, but selling myself for this job would not be easy.

I had a mix of relevant work experience, having been a journalist, starting a nonprofit, and leading political campaigns, so I thought I could make a strong case, but I would definitely be a risky choice, since I'd never run an operation VOX's size.

All I could do was push through my fear and put myself out there. And that's what I'd done, as I hit send on my cover letter:

"There is not a more ideal opportunity for me than helping teens to have a stronger, more powerful voice in Atlanta by helping to lead VOX into its next chapter," I wrote. "It would be thrilling if the next chapter in VOX's story and the next chapter in mine were one in the same."

August 24, 1999

T HE BEST SUMMER job I ever had hit its peak when a simple but jaw-dropping question was shouted to me across the Capital City Stadium press box by the Bombers' media director.

My little booth overlooking the field where the Capital City Bombers played had become my second home during this baseball-filled summer as I covered minor league baseball for *The State*. I always had my notebook, microcassette recorder, and baseball scorebook, so I could score every game—just as Bee had taught me 15 years earlier.

The Bombers were the single-A affiliate of the New York Mets, and typically it was a big deal when top prospects from opposing teams came to face off against the home team. It was a treat to watch and write about future major leaguers like shortstop Rafael Furcal of the Macon Braves, outfielder Matt Holliday of the Asheville Tourists, and former USC star shortstop Brian Roberts of the Delmarva Shorebirds, who'd still been playing for the Gamecocks three months earlier.

But tonight's guest was no prospect.

"Hey Jeff, would you like to interview Tom Seaver?" I thought I heard Mark call out from across the press box.

"Are you serious?" I yelled back, incredulously.

"He'll be here later," Mark said. "I'll come get you."

I wasn't sure how this summer could get much better.

As part of this kick-ass job, I'd already been on assignment to Wrigley Field in Chicago and Fenway Park in Boston. I'd led the coverage of the Major League Baseball draft—which included writing about top high school and college prospects across South Carolina—and I'd spent dozens of afternoons and evenings covering the Bombers.

It was all baseball all the time, but most importantly it was a crash course in storytelling and writing on deadline that made me a real reporter for the first time. But the opportunity to interview one of the best pitchers to ever take the mound took this summer job to another level.

Seaver had won 311 games during his 20-year career with a stellar 2.86 earned run average, while striking out 3,640 hitters. His excellence earned him first-ballot induction into the Baseball Hall of Fame in 1992 with 98.8 percent of the vote, the highest vote percentage by any player ever at the time.

After he'd finished being interviewed on the game's radio broadcast, Seaver and I settled into the sparsely filled bleachers about 20 rows behind home plate and spent the next two innings watching the game and talking pitching.

His main purpose as a roving instructor for the Mets would come in the locker room or on the field with the players after he watched them. "I just pass on anything I can to help," he told me. "Whether it's something that helps them now or five years from now, it's no different."

My work as the Bombers correspondent had begun in March with a feature story assignment on the team's most buzzed-about player, Robert Stratton. Stratton, an outfielder with massive biceps and "light-tower" home run power, had been drafted by the Mets as their first pick in the 1996 draft. On April 9, that story had run as a season preview.

It also served as the most important writing lesson I'd ever received. At just 21, I'd made it through my first five years of journalism without too much editing, so I was beside myself when the edits on the Stratton story came back to me from my editor, Ron, who had written for *Baseball America* and not only knew his baseball but was a talented sportswriter and editor.

"You should probably just put your name on it," I whined to him, showing my age and my ass for the first time since I started working at *The State*.

"Let's take a walk," Ron said calmly, leading me from the newsroom to the downstairs lobby where we sat and talked. My career was changed in that moment.

Ron explained that I had everything there, but it needed to be rearranged a bit and tightened. Writing isn't a solo effort, he told me. Like baseball, it's a team sport, and we can always make each other's work better through collaboration. This was the first of many critical lessons Ron taught me throughout the summer as I grew as a reporter and writer under his experienced baseball-writing eye.

He taught me to look for the story within the game, because baseball writing isn't just about regurgitating play-by-plays, but at its best when we find compelling stories on or off the field.

I embraced this challenge, focusing on finding the story as it happened, rather than making assumptions about what I thought in advance might be the story.

Sometimes I got it right, like in July when I turned a rained-out game into a full story about the need to replace the drainage system at Capital City Stadium. I'd interviewed the team's owner, general manager, and manager while exploring the battle between the team and the Columbia City Council over a $15 million investment in the field.

Other times I got it wrong, like when I quoted an opposing pitcher who had no-hit the Bombers on how he believed God helped him secure his no-hitter. Ron opined that God probably didn't care too much about minor league baseball, and that I should stick to using quotes about the game.

In success and in failure, I would never learn as much, have as much fun, or gain as much confidence as I did covering baseball for *The State* during that summer of 1999.

May 20, 2014

As the numbers began to roll in, it became clear. Elena was going to be the next state senator from DeKalb County, representing District 42. She'd soundly defeated her opponent in the Democratic primary, earning almost 62 percent of the vote.

I couldn't have been prouder of Elena and the team we'd assembled, which included a few members of our 2010 team, like Joe and Liz, along with some new, extremely talented political operatives: my friends Stefan, who served as our finance director, and Matt, who ran the campaign.

While serving House District 81 in 2011 and 2012 following her 2010 victory, Elena had been drawn into the same district with another Democrat during redistricting. She'd decided to avoid a 2012 primary fight with a friend and had instead become a nonprofit executive director, working on consumer protection issues. But when the District 42 Senate seat was vacated in late 2013, Elena had decided that she was ready to return to the legislature and would run for office again.

I was focused on my job at VOX at the time, so my volunteer role was to advise and to help build a team that could achieve victory for Elena, a rare public servant who always works to serve her constituents and community and also embraces the work needed to win tough political campaigns.

In 2012, after I wasn't hired by VOX, Stefan had graciously offered me an office at his law firm in which to work. We had become closer friends in 2013, so I recruited him to lead Elena's fundraising. He was a full-time attorney and hadn't worked on campaigns in years, but he agreed to the role and became an essential friend and my most trusted political collaborator.

I'd gotten to know Matt in 2009 and 2010, when he was the executive director for the Democratic Party of Georgia during Elena's first campaign. Matt had all but retired from politics and was working to launch Xocolatl, a small business specializing in small-batch, fair trade chocolate, when Elena, Stefan, and I met him for lunch in early 2014 to pick his brain about possible candidates to manage the campaign. We were all floored when Matt said he was willing to manage it.

While I began my second year as VOX's executive director, I kept up with the campaign team consistently throughout the winter and spring as we headed toward Election Day. It was such a treat to be in the vicinity of so much political talent. The combination of Elena, Stefan, and Matt was an unstoppable force.

My involvement with Elena's second campaign reminded me that I was at my best when helping to convene a great team but then be a complementary voice, rather than the lead.

It was such a different experience from Elena's first race, since I was only playing a small role—but when she won, the result was just as electrifying.

August 17, 2018

L OSING BEE AND Papa had been devastating.
We'd held a memorial service for Bee and for Papa when
each of them died (Bee on August 9, 2012, and Papa on July 12, 2014),
but today we'd all gathered at Fort Jackson National Cemetery in
Columbia to celebrate them together as they were officially laid to
rest. They'd donated their bodies to USC for medical research, and
now their cremated remains would be united in this place forever,
a little more than four years after their souls had reconnected upon
Papa's death.

Gina, Josh, and their sweet and adorable kids—Jackson, Riley
Cates, and Rutherford—were visiting from England and today's
service had been planned for their visit, so our whole family could
participate. As with most big days in our family, we'd follow this
ceremony with dinner together at Villa Tronco to remember them
and enjoy each other.

Bee and Papa taught us to be kind, to love all people and treat
them equally, to be strong, and to prioritize family.

I don't remember either of them being angry or negative with
any consistency, and they were the most giving and loving people
I'd ever known.

They were our role models and our heroes.

I'll forever remember Papa cooking us breakfast on Christmas morning, and delivering his insightful oratory from the pulpit of Beaver Creek Baptist near Chester after we'd filled up on black pepper-covered gravy biscuits at the Winnsboro Hardee's.

And I'll always remember Bee listening to her Braves on the radio and sharing her writing with me through the hundreds of letters she sent, starting from the time I left for college until her Alzheimer's robbed her of the ability to pen them.

When we were kids, Bee told us her "butterfly stories" to help us fall asleep, and during the day she taught us to play Uno and Rummy, to love puzzles, to strategically hide Easter eggs, and to make sure we older kids included Abby in whatever game we were playing. Each Christmas, we knew we were getting a crisp, 100-dollar bill from them, but not before playing an elaborate game that Bee had created, which was always part-scavenger hunt, part-writing game. And always fun!

In their original memorial services, I'd had the honor of eulogizing them each on behalf of their four grandkids. Today, I didn't prepare remarks on paper. I just spoke from the heart, recounting these memories and others. It was lovely to celebrate Bee and Papa and spend time with everyone, but at dinner, I couldn't stop thinking about two of the biggest regrets of my life.

I was so scared of losing both of them when they were sick that I didn't maximize the time I had to spend with them before they died. I couldn't handle the fact that Bee and I were no longer able to have our weekly phone conversations, and once she was gone, I couldn't fathom the thought of also losing Papa. This fear-based approach to my relationship with each of them had led me to engage differently with them both during their final months than I had throughout my life.

I'd been too self-centered to push through my own fear in order to engage and connect with them in the ways they each deserved.

My failure to be the best grandson I could have been in their final years became a major focus in my 12-Step work. Papa had been gone for a little more than two years, and Bee for a little more than four. I couldn't make amends with either of them. But I could use my recognition of that failure to be a better person now and in the future. I was prepared to make the effort to be a more present and less self-centered son, brother, cousin, nephew, coworker, and friend.

Bee and Papa consistently showed me exactly what to do to embrace our family and to serve others. Now that I was healing and growing through sobriety, I was finally able to think about others instead of myself and work daily to be closer to the person they taught me to be.

June 13, 1994

NEW YORK CITY is the greatest gift my dad ever gave to me. There's a stark difference between being alone and being isolated, and when I'm there, I can experience so many memorable things by myself, while never being isolated from the energy of the living being that is New York.

My love for the city deepens every time I have the good fortune to find myself in its midst—experiencing everything from transformative plays and musicals, to impeccably created meals, to beautifully restored films, to intentionally drawn-out strolls through museums, to sitting on park benches listening to the sounds of taxis and buses and watching New Yorkers buzzing about like lightning bugs, to trips in all directions through the labyrinth of trains beneath and above the city. Everything I love doing there can be done alone or with others, and except for baseball games, I've done all the things I love to do there both ways.

I was 16 when Dad, Mom, Bryan, and I landed at LaGuardia for the first time on Friday, June 10, 1994, the day before Bryan's 12th birthday. As we rode in the taxi toward the island of Manhattan, it seemed more massive than I'd expected, with the majestic twin towers of the World Trade Center rising high to our left at Manhattan's southern tip and the Empire State Building, in midtown, on the horizon to our right.

Dad had booked us a room at the Essex House hotel on Central Park South, across the street from the southern end of Central Park and just down the block from famous sites like FAO Schwarz—the toy store we knew from watching Tom Hanks and Robert Loggia hop and dance on the giant floor piano in *Big*—and The Plaza Hotel, which we remembered from *Home Alone 2: Lost in New York*.

During that first trip, we ate brunch at The Plaza, scarfed down massive pastrami sandwiches and slices of cheesecake just as tall from Carnegie Deli, and devoured burgers at Mickey Mantle's Restaurant & Sports Bar, a block east of our hotel. We got more than we bargained for there when the legendary switch-hitting Yankee Hall of Famer visited tables after he finished recording a radio show in the back of the restaurant. "How are the burgers?" the Mick asked us, as he briefly paused at our table. My mouth was full of fries and seized with anxiety, so I just nodded as he told us to enjoy our meal and New York. Then he moved on, greeting every table in the vicinity of the radio booth before he left.

Mickey's old team was on the road in Canada playing the Blue Jays, so I wouldn't experience Yankee Stadium until seven years later. But we made it to Shea Stadium in Queens on Sunday afternoon to watch the Mets beat Canada's other team, the Montreal Expos, 5–4 on a Kevin McReynolds solo homer in the bottom of the eighth—all the while hearing planes flying in and out of nearby LaGuardia rumble overhead every few minutes.

The night before, we'd gone together to the St. James Theater on West 44th Street to see *The Who's Tommy*. My first Broadway show was an unforgettable experience.

I was totally immersed in the lights and sounds of the rock musical that had won five Tony Awards the previous year by telling the story of the newfound stardom of Tommy, the deaf, dumb, and blind Pinball Wizard.

Mom and I also broke off from Dad and Bryan during the trip to see *Grease* at the Eugene O'Neill Theater on West 49th Street, which was starring Rosie O'Donnell as Rizzo. It wasn't a sensory fireworks show like *Tommy*, but after having memorized most of the John Travolta–Olivia Newton-John movie by repeatedly watching the VHS recording during the 1980s, it was fun to see the story play out on the stage.

On Monday, June 13, as we packed up to head back to Columbia, I heard the heartbreaking news on *SportsCenter* that Ryne Sandberg was retiring. It was an off day for the Cubs, but a special news conference had been called to announce that the 34-year-old former MVP had decided to walk away from the remaining $15 million on his contract.

"The things that made me a great player have left me," Sandberg told the press that day. "That edge, the drive, the killer instinct. It ended up taking me two-and-a-half months to realize it. I was thinking it would come back. It never did."

I missed Sandberg's final game the Friday before at Wrigley, which I would have watched had we been home. But I couldn't stop thinking about my first New York adventure. I thought I'd never see my baseball hero take the field again, which was sad, but I knew for sure I'd return to New York.

November 29, 2017

I HAD NEVER WANTED to die as much as I did in this moment. The starkest example in my life—my dad's suicide—about what to do in this situation was telling me to do exactly that. Die.

Ideas and thoughts of suicide were often present in my mind, but never as vividly as they were right now.

I pictured a heavy noose around my neck as I fell forward off my third-floor balcony.

I imagined inserting a razor blade into my wrist and pulling down vertically to rip open my left arm.

I envisioned a handgun against my right temple with my finger on the trigger.

I had none of the tools needed to execute these ideas.

I had only my broken mind and heart—both in a bottomless freefall—and a sharp knife, a bathtub, and my worst impulses.

I'd been fired from a campaign earlier in the day—the only time I'd ever been fired in my life—and was given the feedback that I'd been inappropriate with women, but I wasn't given much more information than that. With less than a week to Election Day, my candidate couldn't risk his campaign on my drunken failures.

The political adviser in me agreed with him unequivocally; my scared human self was lost, searching for answers and direction.

Somehow, that night, I essentially ended the life I had built over the past 10 years without actually becoming my own executioner.

To stay alive, I talked to a couple of friends—not telling them the disturbing nature of my suicidal thoughts. And I hid in my bed watching *Survivor* while I tried to figure out how to survive my own mind. The increasingly destructive role alcohol had played in my life as my drinking became more excessive and intertwined with anxiety, depression, and suicidal ideas was inescapable.

Over the preceding three years, my alcohol consumption had accelerated as my marriage crumbled. Drinking then became a serious problem as I tried to navigate the emotional untethering from my 13-year union. I had chosen divorce, but only with hopes of finding happiness and true emotional intimacy with someone else; not to drunkenly hit on several friends. But when I was lonely and sad with bourbon in my blood, I'd acted in ways that I never would have when sober.

The opposite of addiction is connection, which, deep down, was what I was searching for when making unsolicited advances. But it didn't come across that way. I'd disrespected my friends. I felt deep shame. And I knew that alcohol was fueling my toxic behavior.

For the past two years, the person I wanted to be and the person I was being daily had been completely disconnected from each other. I was deeply insecure, and felt alone and unappreciated. Without the stabilizing effect of marriage to keep them in check, those neuroses were forcing their way into my every human interaction, whether I was under the influence of alcohol or not.

I drank socially to soften my social anxiety. Over time, the amount I'd had to drink socially had been increasing, but even after my divorce in 2015 and 2016, I was only drinking excessively a handful of times on a monthly basis. But by late 2017, if I was drinking, it was to excess.

On those nights that I was out and Robinson was with Audrey, I would drink—a lot—and drive. I would send flirty texts to friends.

And I would misread in-person situations and ask out or flirt with female friends. The sober me never wanted to disrespect or offend anyone, but when I drank, I did just that.

Because I didn't drink at home, and because I thought I'd spent so much of my life as a responsible drinker, it didn't occur to me for a long time that I might be an alcoholic. But I was facing an inescapable choice: I could continue with the post-divorce version of myself—driven by deep fears of isolation only exacerbated by brown liquor—and follow my dad's example, letting my pain, shame, and fear drive me to suicide. *Or* I could respect the feedback I'd received, own my failures, ask for help, and commit myself to being the man that in my heart I wanted to be.

I knew the unspeakable damage that suicide can do to so many people who are left behind. And so, as I hid in my bed fighting off the life-ending ideation demons, I chose differently.

I chose life. I chose change. I chose sobriety.

And I chose correctly.

July 29, 2020

I DON'T KNOW WHY I turned right on Peachtree Street to head downtown. Usually, I'd take Courtland down to the Capitol. But sometimes my subconscious knows better.

The reason for this route became clear quickly.

Soon, on the right, I passed Emory Midtown, where my tongue cancer had been excised in April 2018.

Across the street on the left was St. Luke's Episcopal, where I'd been confirmed in 2017, and where I'd prayed for the strength to beat cancer before my surgery.

As I made my way toward the intersection of Peachtree Street and Andrew Young International Boulevard, it hit me: I was driving through monuments of my past life.

Peachtree Center, to my left, was where I'd been executive director of VOX from 2013 to 2017, and where my emotions had run the full gamut, from passion to pride to pain. It was where I'd absorbed myriad lessons I needed to learn about leadership, management, patience, respect, grace, honesty, vulnerability, and course-correction.

On the same corner as Peachtree Center was Hard Rock Café, where my dad used to take us when we went into town for Braves games in the late 1980s and early 1990s.

Then, as I crossed Ellis Street and came upon Woodruff Park, I realized I would soon cross through Five Points, the heart of innovation in Atlanta (Coca-Cola was first served there at Jacobs Pharmacy in 1886). It had also been the namesake for my failed consulting firm, Five Points Civic Strategies, where I'd hoped to impact the community through political and nonprofit work, but instead had been crushed by the wreckage of my alcoholism.

As I turned left on Trinity Avenue, I felt the pulses of panic and fear begin working to keep me driving. I overcame them and parked, so that I could pay my respects to Congressman John Lewis, who had taught us to set aside race, class, age, language, sexual orientation, nationality, religious affiliation, and gender identity to demand unequivocal respect for human dignity.

I awoke this morning to find a 5 a.m. group text message from Rachelle, a longtime aide to Mr. Lewis, inviting me and others who had worked on his campaigns and in his office to come to the Georgia State Capitol building to each sit for a 30-minute shift, as part of a six-hour vigil.

This man, a hero to me and to countless people, had fought and bled to create "good trouble" in service of the moral obligation to stand up and speak out against injustice.

After parking and starting my three-block walk, my still-lurking fears somehow melted away the closer I was to the Gold Dome, where Congressman Lewis was lying in state. A seemingly endless line of masked mourners was braving the pandemic to spend a few moments at his casket.

Black. White. Brown. They loved John Lewis.

They came in ripped jeans and expensive suits and Black Lives Matter shirts and John Lewis gear.

I even saw the iconic T-shirt with the Congressman's mugshot on it that had been designed by my friend Bess.

My fears were replaced by humility and gratitude to be among the former campaign and legislative staffers, interns, and volunteers who had been invited to sit in rotating 30-minute vigils in groups of six, on the opposite side of the American flag-draped casket from the line of mourners. Bess was sitting a seat away from me beside her brother, Matt, who had been the Congressman's (and Elena's) former campaign manager. Somehow, as I sat there and prayed, I was at peace for the first time in longer than I could remember.

For almost 25 years, I had been living a life ruled by fears stemming from my father's suicide. I'd fought to prove myself because I never was good enough for him. Sometimes this had driven me to achieve success; but, mixed with alcohol, it had turned me into an insecure, toxic prick who wore his unprocessed emotions on his sleeve, had a compulsive need to brag about his successes, and acted as if he knew it all.

"Believe in me," I had begged people with my actions, because I sure as hell hadn't believed in myself. When I didn't feel appreciated, I'd told myself that not valuing my work was proof that those people or that person clearly agreed that I was as worthless as I believed myself to be.

If I weren't worthless, wouldn't Dad have gotten out of that Volvo?

In active alcoholism, I could never hide that pain, even without a drop of liquor in my boiling blood.

I'd exuded it.

It had been written on my face and present in my voice. Deep sorrow, projected as aggression and anger.

All I'd wanted was to be loved and appreciated, but my fear- and anxiety-driven behavior and reactions had virtually ensured the opposite would be my seemingly never-ending reality.

Ironically, my fight to keep from following my father's example of suicide had been killing the best version of myself.

But as I sat there thinking about the life of service lived by Congressman Lewis, it didn't matter that I had previously approached my life in such a negative way. It didn't matter that I hadn't been in this building since November 27, 2017. It didn't matter that, two days after that, I had almost ended my life. And it didn't matter how much my life had changed through sobriety since 2017.

All that mattered was Mr. Lewis, and how he'd impacted our world. As I sat there, I only thought of him. I prayed for him and for his family, friends, and the people across the world who loved him. I remembered his sacrifices and reflected on his impact as a hero of the world.

Driving home, I began to connect my experience celebrating the Congressman's lifetime of service to my own failures.

For so much of my life, my now-diagnosed anxieties and clinical depression had manifested themselves in extreme selfishness, and in deep fears that always led me away from the person I dreamed of being.

Mr. Lewis was a hero of mine because of how he was able to live a selfless life in service of others.

I wanted to serve others, but insecurity, fear, and anxiety had prevented me from feeling worthy enough to do so without getting in my own way. Instead, they'd each wreaked havoc on my life, especially when mixed with alcohol.

I'd found myself aggressively arguing with colleagues when I all truly wanted was to collaborate and create positive impact together.

I'd found myself drunk in public, making inappropriate advances toward female friends in a misplaced desire for emotional connection.

I'd found myself unable to leave my bed for days because I'd leaned into my depression and self-centeredness instead of dedicating myself to serving and engaging with others.

I'd found myself a world away from the person I had the promise of being at 27 years old, when I first met Mr. Lewis in the sanctuary of 16th Street Baptist Church in Birmingham on March 4, 2005.

And then I'd found my life in free fall, and my father's final choice came into focus as my solution.

Would I follow his example of suicide, or would I hear the universe urging me to find help? Would I overcome the guilt and shame of failing to be the man I envisioned? Would I actually find help? Would I seek and discover true growth? Would I be forgiven for my failures? Would I forgive myself?

Would I choose to live, or conclude my story?

On Thursday November 30, 2017, I had awakened. I was alive.

That morning, I committed myself to live, learn, and dedicate my life to becoming the man I knew I could be.

My next chapter had begun when I formally asked for help by accepting that white chip, AA, and the fellowship that came with it, as I left that meeting with Jason in Charlotte on December 3, 2017, to return to Atlanta and face my failures.

Today, as I rested my hand on the flag covering the Congressman's casket in the rotunda of the Georgia Capitol, I remembered sitting across from him during lunch at J. R. Crickets on Cascade in 2008. He didn't talk about himself. He talked about the people who fought alongside him during the Civil Rights Movement.

He taught me that getting in the way isn't about one person. Service is about others.

I was fortunate enough to have a rare audience with an American hero, but I failed to internalize his stories and integrate their lessons into my life.

I realized now, at 42, that so much of my life—guided as it was by fear, anxiety, and a need to prove myself and feel appreciated—had been in service of myself.

If I had followed in my dad's footsteps, my story would have mirrored his, and I would have just been a selfish boy who became a selfish man and made a selfish final choice. But I know now that my first true act in service to others was choosing not to set off the domino effect of suicide-based emotional chaos that had rippled across my own existence since February 24, 1996.

I realized my life had become unmanageable, and I admitted that I was powerless over alcohol—and over anxiety, fear, and depression, and the scars from my relationship with my dad and my trauma journey from his suicide. So, I committed myself to a sober life centered around serving others. This lofty ideal of service is one to which I strive daily, but it's not yet as seamless as I hope it will be, thanks to my realizations as I reflected on Mr. Lewis's life and death.

Now I see that I was always on a journey to this moment, when I could finally see clearly and commit myself to overcoming fear and negativity to live a more positive life, striving to reach a fraction of the ideals exemplified by the actions of my heroes, Clyde and Vera Riley and Congressman John Lewis.

Today, I was given one of the great opportunities of my life, as I said goodbye to Mr. Lewis alongside old friends. In turn, my life moving forward will be rooted in service to others as he taught us all, through his daily philosophies, impact, and example.

February 24, 2021

S TEVE ROMIG DIED 25 years ago this morning.
That's such a crazy sentence to write, not only because it
feels like it can't have been 25 years, but also because a version of
him has been whispering in my ear for that long.

I recently re-read the letter he wrote me the night before he
ended his life, and my 2020 reading of it led to some big revelations.

First off, I'm incredibly grateful that he decided to write letters.
Countless suicide survivors receive no answers or insights to why
their loved one chose to die by suicide. In sobriety, I've built a gratitude practice for the first time in my life, and I was still surprised by
feeling grateful to have these words and answers after re-reading his
letter.

Second, it's the perfect example of the idea that our trauma is
the constant and we are the variable in our journey to live with and
attempt to recover from our traumatic experiences. Regardless of its
content, I'm grateful to have this piece of paper, which he printed
and placed in its envelope before I held it in my 18-year-old hands
and read it, through my tears and fury, that morning in 1996.

In myriad ways I'm a different person from the high school kid
who read it at 18, the college graduate who read it at 22, and the

married guy who read it at 27. I used to read it annually around his anniversary, to see how my view of the world and my lived experiences had changed my interpretation of what I was reading. But I stopped doing that sometime before I turned 30.

There are some phrases I'll never forget. And I was actually surprised—when I revisited his words in 2020 as a divorced, 42-year-old recovering alcoholic—by things he'd written but that I'd forgotten. But I was also able to hear his words to me differently and, frankly, in a more adult and less angry way.

He was so sure of himself, so sure of the advice he was giving me, and so sure of the decision he'd made to leave.

It's impossible to picture what my life might have been like, had he made an alternate choice. While I, of course, don't agree at all with his decision to end his life, I can now find comfort in his belief that he was doing what was best for his family.

And I can appreciate that, despite talking to no one as he made this final decision, he found the ability to talk to us in the only way he was able—through his letters.

When we lose a loved one to suicide, it's natural for their final act and the trauma that ensues to be their sole legacy.

But in writing this memoir, I've been able to reconnect with my dad in so many ways, through the memories of people who knew him and by digging deeper in my mind to reclaim memories with which I'd lost touch.

As I remember him today, I remember how smart he was, and how he always greeted people with his broad, welcoming smile.

I remember how talented he was at tennis and at shooting pool, and I wish I'd inherited the discipline he was able to tap into to excel at sports, academics, and bankruptcy law.

I remember him teaching me how to change a tire and how to drive a manual transmission, which remains the only kind of car I'll ever purchase.

I remember that he introduced me to New York City and took us on fun adventures to Colorado and Chichen Itza, to Disney World and the Caribbean.

Until his last breath, he made what he believed was the right decision: to take care of us.

In my mind, he did a great job in his relationship with my brother. Dad was ever the accomplished student, and I believe he learned from his first parenting experience dealing with a jackass teenager, and built a great relationship with Bryan, who, four years and four months younger than me, was a far sweeter, kinder, and easier kid.

I'm eternally grateful for their relationship, which is proof to me that so many times, he got it right, whether or not I was able to see that in my teens, my twenties, or my thirties.

Now, I want to remember him as a whole human, with the flaws I understand better now, as a 43-year-old who struggles with similar mental health challenges.

I appreciate my dad for everything he continues to teach me. I will continue to learn from his life and his death as I work to live a healthier, more positive life in service of others, rather than in service to self.

In his memory, I reiterate my commitment to living life, and to learning from my experiences.

I'll stay alive as an example for others who share our mental health struggles, and I'll stay alive for those who love me.

Because I now actually believe that the concept of others loving me is plausible, and I'm working to join them by loving myself and believing in my own worthiness, in ways that allow me to love them and to let them love me.

Each and every human is worthy of living life while taking responsibility for their actions and embracing the opportunities given to learn, to grow, and to evolve into better versions of themselves. This version of me is a man who will respect women in all circumstances, support the LGBTQIA+ community, and maintain a commitment to anti-racism and racial equity. My best self will also support other alcoholics as they work to stay sober and is dedicated to making the world a better place through all his daily efforts, personally and professionally.

But the only way we can become the best versions of ourselves is to look critically at every area of our lives where we want to improve, name those things, and strive daily to be better.

We all have successes. We all have failures. And believe it or not, we can all fill a book with memories and stories about our passions, people, and experiences.

Remembering your own stories is what I hope this book will do for you. I don't expect you to write your own book, and I don't expect your propensity for suicidal thoughts to evaporate when you close this book. Mine hasn't.

Thinking about suicide is natural and likely for people who struggle with mental illness. You might think about ropes or razors. Or maybe you count barbiturates or bullets. Or you may envision drowning in a body of water or dying while trapped in a car filled with carbon monoxide.

But ideation isn't execution, and NEVER has to be.

I hope my stories have connected you with yours, and I hope you realize as you finish this book that regardless of what your mind is telling you, you are OK, and you can build from that.

Writing a book did not fix me. I still struggle every day, but now I've found a new ability to connect to my passions, people, and experiences to help me push through darkness.

I don't have a silver bullet that will cure you or me of anxiety, depression, or suicidal ideation. But I hope you can now accept what I've been able to recently understand.

We are valuable. We are worthy. We are loved.

And if we stay alive, we can have the future of which we dream and find the connection we crave.

It won't be easy, but it will be worth it. For you, and for me.

In AA, we say *move a muscle, change a thought.*

So, move. Change. Go.

Go push through the pain and panic and paralysis to remember your passions, people, and experiences.

Go succeed. Go fail. Go learn. Go create new memories. Go change the world.

Just. Keep. Going.

Stay alive.

And I will, too.

EPILOGUE

August 21, 2021

TODAY WAS ONE of those days when I was deeply grateful I'd stayed alive to experience its magic.

When we're in our darkest moments, we tend to forget these days, but they're the ones in which we should anchor our minds as we fight through our suicidal ideation to stay alive.

Nevertheless, today was all about ghosts. Some had died recently and naturally. Some had died long ago and prematurely. And at least had one died at his own hands on February 24, 1996.

As we gathered in the cemetery, I realized I'd never seen so many Romigs in one place as the names of my ancestors adorned headstone after headstone in the family plot at St. Paul's United Church of Christ in Trexlertown, Pennsylvania.

Even though my dad had never been to this place, his spirit was more palpable to me at this moment than I could ever remember. And, for the first time since a July 1991 trip to New Albany, Indiana, all of the Romig cousins—along with my aunt Joan and uncle

Wayne—had traveled to this spot in rural Lehigh County to say goodbye to our grandparents.

Ruth had died on January 3, 2020, and then Clarence had passed away on May 20, 2021.

The pandemic had prevented us from gathering to remember Ruth in the immediate wake of her death, but it was fitting that their ashes were sharing space in the beautifully hand-carved, wooden box Joan had created. Today, after almost 70 years together in life, they were reunited and buried together in the same county where Clarence had grown up.

Clarence was born in East Texas, Pennsylvania on February 2, 1929, and had met Ruth while serving in the United States Army in Berlin. She was born in Berlin on July 4, 1931, grew up there during the horrors of World War II, and gave birth to my father on November 4, 1948.

Even though the war was over when dad was born, Berlin was not yet a peaceful place, according to a letter Ruth wrote in February 2006, reflecting about my dad for the tenth anniversary of his death. "Very few things were normal in that time period and in that part of the world," she wrote.

World War II had been over for three years and the four Allied Powers—the United States, Great Britain, the Soviet Union, and France—had divided Germany into four zones, each occupied by one of the Allied Powers. Berlin was in the midst of the Russian zone and was likewise divided into four sectors. In a political effort to force the three western allies to leave Berlin, the Russians blockaded the city in the fall of 1948.

"This required the three western allies to create an airlift to bring food, coal, and other supplies for the trapped occupying forces and the German population," Ruth remembered in her letter. "Steven was born in the middle of that war-like mess, during one of the daily power outages. He was brought home to his German grandmother's two-story house on a secluded street near the southern border of the American sector of Berlin."

Joan was born in August 1954, almost six years after her big brother Steve, with Wayne rounding out their Romig family in September 1955. Today, as part of paying our respects to Ruth and Clarence, Joan had arranged two incredibly special field trips for us. For lunch, we ate at the 1760 Pub in Trexlertown, which has not only been around since 1760, but was made possible, in part, by Frederick Romich—our direct ancestor, who would change the spelling of our name to Romig—who joined five others to vouch for pub owner John Trexler in a petition to King George that was needed to procure the license to open a tavern house.

Then, after a hearty lunch of fish and chips at the pub, where sports-filled 70-inch high-definition televisions hang on the original 1760 walls, we drove about 25 miles to tour the land where Frederick's father, Johann Adam Romich, had built a log cabin in 1733 when he brought his wife and eight children to America from the small village of Ittlingen, Germany, which sits about 40 kilometers southeast of Heidelberg and at last count had fewer than 2,500 residents.

The current property owner, Fritz, had grown up on the land, which is now primarily a soybean farm. Joan had originally connected with Fritz in 1998 to visit the original Romich homestead, which added a large stone house in 1760 that is today occupied by Fritz's daughter.

The walking tour of the property left me literally breathless from all the uphill hiking and figuratively so from experiencing this deep connection to my Romig ancestry which I'd never taken the time to explore, despite knowing of the work Joan had been doing since the late 1990s to understand the roots of our family.

Dad never knew any of this either. He never seemed to have much interest in the deep German heritage on both sides of our Romig family. He and Clarence had had a rocky relationship when Dad was growing up, not unlike my relationship with him, I suppose, or Clarence's with his father, Arlan, an alcoholic who died at the age of 49.

In a lovely conversation with Wayne after tonight's dinner at the Deitsch Eck Restaurant in Lenhartsville, he shared with me that Clarence's approach to life—very strict, a focus on education, workaholism—stemmed from experiencing his father's alcoholism and inability to hold a steady job. As we talked about the father-son dynamics over at least three generations of our family's history, I realized that Steve and I were part of a larger generational cycle that neither of us really understood as we drifted apart between the late 1980s and his 1996 death.

In Grandma's letter from 2006, she told a story that reflected on Dad's relationship with his father and easily could have been a roles-reversed story from my teen years. During the summer of 1965, they were living in Lanham, Maryland, when Clarence nagged 17-year-old Steve to get involved with something in the community, rather than sit around the apartment.

"Steve, do you think someone is going to knock on that door and invite you to come outside and do something?" Ruth remembered Clarence asking him. "Immediately after that loud and strong question, someone [the pool manager] did knock on the door and offered Steven a paying job as a lifeguard in the apartment complex pool."

Unfortunately, when we were growing up, because of their father-son dynamic, Dad maintained distance from his parents. They had settled in Urbana, Illinois, so Clarence could teach at the University of Illinois, and lived there until they each died. That distance from my grandparents extended to us as well. But, despite this friction, we did take two memorable trips to spend time with our Romig family when I was growing up. Two years before we spent our July 1993 week in Colorado with Joan, Ron, Annaliese, and Eric, we all met at Wayne's house in New Albany (a suburb of Louisville, Kentucky) to celebrate Ruth's 60th birthday on July 4, 1991.

Wayne's boys were so little then. The twins, Brent and Warren, had turned one just a week earlier, and Cameron was almost two-and-a-half. Eric was only five-and-a-half, Annaliese was almost seven-and-a-half, and Bryan had just turned nine in June. At 13, I was the oldest and the only one with any real memories of the 1991 trip, which was clear as we became reacquainted as adults in the Trexlerville cemetery alongside Joan, Wayne, Annaliese's husband Daniel, and Bryan's wife Beth.

My memories from that 1991 trip include grandma blowing out her birthday candles, sneaking off to watch *Days of Our Lives*, and dad taking me to the July 5 Triple-A baseball game between the Louisville Cardinals and the Columbus Clippers, the Yankees' top minor league team at the time. Kevin Mmahat, Columbus' starting pitcher, no-hit the Cardinals that day, winning 6-0. It's still the only no-hitter I've ever seen in person, but most importantly it was the only time my dad and I took a one-on-one trip to a baseball game. I still have the ticket from that day.

Dad's relationship with his mom always seemed better some-how, and it was mind-blowing to hear his voice for the first time in more than 25 years on an audio cassette recording he made for Ruth shortly before 8 a.m. on Oct. 31, 1978. Joan found these tapes in grandma's boxes, digitized the audio, and sent three priceless recordings to Bryan and me just days before this trip.

"Jeffrey has grown and grown and grown," dad says into the dic-tating machine from his law office that he'd brought home to our house in North Augusta. "His hair has come out. His eyes are still blue, and he scoots around so quickly. You really have to watch what he'll get into."

Dad told Grandma about Mom's recently-acquired cross-stitch-ing hobby, shared about the new carpet and wallpaper in his law office that he'd received compliments on, talked about Bee going back to school to get her master's degree, talked about Papa getting the deed to part of the land he grew up on outside of Columbia and their plans to build a new house in the country, and described the 1977 Volkswagen Rabbit he'd recently bought used and how much he enjoyed it.

"It had 19,000 miles on it, but it was just in beautiful condition," he told her in his surprisingly pronounced Southern accent. "I just love it. The performance is super. I just decided I needed something with air conditioning. It's a bright red, and it's got a little racing stripe down the side that says Rabbit on it. Sandra thought it was kind of racy for a lawyer to have. But she's driven it. She loves it just as well. In fact, we have disagreements as to who's going to drive it."

Throughout Steve's dictation, I'm fighting for his attention. "Da, Da, Da, Da, Da," I coo.

"What's the matter, Jeffrey? It's my turn to talk. I am talking right now, Jeffrey," he sweetly joked with his eight-month-old co-star. "You don't have to hog the mic. Oh, you just want to be held. I tell you what, a baby is sure demanding. Always something. I spend time with him in the morning and again in the evening. We have a real good relationship. He's just exploring."

When I told mom about this now-digitized audio file Joan had made from the original cassette she found, she said that was a consistent routine for Dad and me when I was a baby. "He used to play with you early in the morning like that," she told me. "He'd let me sleep in, and he'd feed you and spend time with you."

This recording, made more than 17 years before his death, was a stark contrast from the words in his suicide letter, which until listening to this audio, were his last words to me.

I never felt closer to my father as I listened to the kindness and love and patience in his voice as he multi-tasks making this taped letter for his mom and chasing me early in the morning of Halloween 1978. And, today, in Pennsylvania, I felt a different connection to Dad, as I realized I wasn't only here representing myself as we toured the land on which our family settled in 1732.

For the first time in more than 25 years, I truly embraced my role as Steve's oldest son, and when I thanked Fritz for our tour, I made a point to do so on behalf of my dad as well.

Suicide kept Steve from these experiences. Luckily, avoiding my own suicide allowed me to understand him, myself, and our family on a deeper level than I'd ever anticipated.

It's amazing what's possible if we fight through our suicidal ideas and just fucking stay alive.

DFKY Donors

Aaron Boyd

Abbie Chaddick

Abby Tennenbaum

Alan Richard

Alex Seblatnigg

Alice Rolls & Melissa Nunnick

Alok Deshpande

Amanda Rhein

Amanda Kay Seals

Amber Suitt

Amir Farokhi & Julie Okada

Amol & Trish Naik

Ana Maria Paramo

Ann Cramer

Annaliese Reed Fay

Andrew Dietz

Andrew Sprouse

Andy Deutsch & Lauren Estrin

Andy Phelan

Ann Kennedy

Anne Simone

Anthony & Wendy Roth
Cimino

April Atkins

Ashley Krieg Byrd

Ashley Parks

Bailey Garrot

Becca Posey

Ben & JJ Getz

Ben Miller

Ben Spears

Bess Weyandt

Bharath Parthasarathy

Brandon Carl

Brandon George

Brian Fisher

Bryan & Beth Romig

Bryan Talbert

Callie Roan

Carla Smith

Carmen Sanchez

Caroline & Jeff DiBattisto

Carson Sowell Twombley
Catherine Woodling
Charleston Woodworking
School
Chris & Annie Appleton
Chris Harrison
Chris & Tina McDonald
Cicely Garrett
Clarence Romig
Corinne Kocher
Dan Goldberg
Dan Gordon
David & Barbara Tennenbaum
Doug Shipman
Elaine Hudson & David Guy
Elena Parent & Briley
Brisendine
Ellen Hunter
Elizabeth Shara
Ellen Mendelsohn Klasson
Emily & Trace Hawkins
Emily & Zachary Hennessee
Emily Tudor Strickland
Eric Teusink
Erin & Richmond Bernhardt
Erin Glynn
Erin & Byron Kirkpatrick
Erin & Jordan Wakefield
Fabiola Charles Stokes
Geneva Hall-Shelton
Gina & Josh Rieger
Glenn Fosnacht
Greg Bluestein

Greg Clay
Greg & Sherri Peterman
Heather Boyd Sharp
Hilary King
Holly Smith
Howard Franklin
Hunter Pierson
Jackie Smith
Jaci Bertrand
Jane Bradshaw Burnette
Jane Kidd
Jared Jones
Jason & Alicia Allman
Jason & Ariel Esteves
Jason Smith
Jen Moll
Jenna Mobley
Jennifer Spring
Jibran Shermohammed
Jill Johnson Wandstrat
Jim Burress
Jim Pallotta
Jimmy Trimble
Joan & Ron Reed
Joel Feldman
Joel Mendelson
John & Debi Bailey
John Hardman
John Noel
Judith Winfrey & Joe Reynolds
Julianna Cagle
Karen DeFilippi
Kate Atwood

Kate Carter
Kate Sandhaus
Katherine Gatza Zenus
Katie Beasley
Katie King
Katie Long
Kim Karris
Kristina Christy
Kristin Kim
Lana & Steve Hefner
Lara Smith
Laura Hamm
Leslie Herman & Joshua Smith
Lindsey Kirshner
Lindsey Knox & Joel Williams
Linsay Crosby Rohr
Madden Manion
Madison Roberts
Mandy Mahoney
Marci Robinson Saltzman
Mariana Pinango
Mario Cambardella
Mart Martin
Maru Gonzalez
Mary Anne Calamas Painter
Mary Browning Marek
Mary Howell
Matt Weiss
Megan Holder & Dan Chandler
Melissa Gimbel Spearman
Melissa & Adam Jackson
Meredith Jones Jaggard
Michele Medori

Michelle Asbill Jowers
Michelle Hiskey
Mijha & Runako Godfrey
Mike Fitzgerald
Mindy Kao
Molly Chase
Nancy Leavenworth
Natalie Cook
Natalie Woodward
Nichole Fields
Nora Benavidez
Odette Yousef
Pam Cates
Perri & Donn Cooper
Rachael Gandy
Rachel Ezzo
Rachel Alterman Wallack
Rachel Fox Weitz
Rebecca Kaye
Rob Teilhet
Ron & Mary Carolyn Thigpen
Ryan King
Sam & Ann Nicole Sprouse
Sandra & Chuck Lawson
Sara Forman
Sarah Ambrose
Sarah Lytle Kistler
Shannon Pinel Johnson
Shannon Makaila
Sonja & Carl Muckenfuss
Spencer Baker
Staci Fox
Stanley & Shannon Romanstein

Stephanie Gerdes

Stephanie Rachmeler

Stephanie Stuckey

Stephanie Tanner

Stephanie Turgeon

Steve Clyburn

Steve & Melissa Reba

Susan Landrum

Suzanne Girdner

Tim Harmon

Todd Money

Tony & Kay Casey

Tracey Robinson

Valerie Cox

Walt & Cookie Sprouse

Wayne Romig

Whitney Deal Marshall

Will & Mareasa Rooks

Will Sellers

Zac McCrary

Acknowledgments

DFKY wouldn't have been possible without the love, support, contributions, and impact of the following:

Mom and Bryan, for your unwavering love and support, and our extended family—Rileys, Lawsons, Romigs, Cates, Riegers, Bryants, Boyds, Petermans, Muckenfusses, Boyds, Robbinses, D'Allesios, Uptons, Kordonises, Romansteins, Jamisons, Reeds, and Fays—especially Pam, Wally, Gina, Abby, and of course, Bee and Papa Riley.

Jason, my best friend since we were kids, for always being there, but especially for helping to save my life by introducing me to Alcoholics Anonymous.

Bill W., Dr. Bob, and every alcoholic with whom I've connected in the rooms and Zooms of AA since 2017, especially my sponsor Jesse, who works the best program of anyone I know, and Lindsey, the best sober friend I could've ever imagined.

Melanie, my DFKY teammate and marketing guru; Megan, my dear friend and original DFKY title designer; and my talented and dedicated editors, including Jodi, Gresham, Aja, and the wonderful folks at Scribe.

Alexis, not only for your editing and friendship, but for allowing me to quote dialogue from your exquisite play *Wanda, Daisy & the Great Rapture*. I can't wait for it to be a movie!

Alan, for your pro bono editing, and for being a dedicated friend since 2000.

Lane, my mentor and writing coach, who treated me like a peer from the moment we met and gave me the confidence to face off against so many fears to actually write and share my stories with the world.

Amir, Elena, Mijha, Aaron, Stefan, Joshua, Leslie, and Don, for always believing in me.

Amber, Caroline, and Mary Elizabeth, who each helped me stay relatively sane on a daily basis as I wrote this book.

My work families from *The Viking Shield*, *The Gamecock*, *The State*, the *Herald-Journal*, the *South Bend Tribune*, Involvement through News & Civics, VOX Teen Communications, Georgia Organics, and all my political teams. I wouldn't be the storyteller, leader, or person I am without your impact on me during the past 25 years.

Hayley, for showing me more of New York than I would have ever found on my own and for being a steadfast friend while doing it.

Dr. Spring, for helping me manage my anxiety, depression, and suicidal ideas.

Robinson and Sandberg, for showing me what unconditional love is.

Made in the USA
Coppell, TX
04 August 2023